ASIA ON THE MOVE

ASIA ON THE MOVE

POPULATION PRESSURE, MIGRATION, AND RESETTLEMENT
IN EASTERN ASIA UNDER THE INFLUENCE OF WANT AND WAR

BRUNO LASKER

Issued under the auspices of the
American Council, Institute of Pacific Relations

NEW YORK: HENRY HOLT AND COMPANY

FOREWORD

THE AGENDA OF PEACE to which this volume is contributed as a modest compendium has its immediate and its more distant objectives. A cry of distress rises from many lands; everywhere the homeless and the disinherited are entitled to such aid as the world community can render them generously and without delay. But there is need also for joint efforts that go beyond the immediate tasks of relief and rehabilitation, efforts unprecedented in their magnitude. We must gird ourselves for jobs in human engineering that require scientific precision and with it the courage to abandon some of the old reliances on narrowly conceived measures of national protection. There will be no room for prejudice. Self-interest will have to be re-interpreted in the terms of a new interdependence of peoples. For, the circumstances which we now confront were alien to the thinking of our fathers. Technical progress has brought about a new mobility of body and mind that cannot be kept within national or even regional bounds, but must, for good or ill, be utilized as a global force. Some see in this new mobility a threatening source of strife. But that it need not be if we but will enlarge our outlook in keeping with our new mastery of distance. It need not be if we will recognize the community of our purposes with those of other peoples. Neither the dislocation of population groups nor the flow of migration from areas of misfortune to areas of opportunity concerns only the governments immediately responsible for the welfare of those affected. Emigration and immigration, even the internal redistribution of population, in so far as it changes the character of a national economy and its role in world economy, cease to be matters of solely "domestic" concern. By concerted planning between nations the new mobility may yet become another link of strength in their common striving for a durable peace.

The present study has for its subject the movements of population in one part of the world, eastern Asia. It attempts to give just enough historical background to help the reader recognize recent drifts as parts of a continuing process, a process partly determined by natural conditions and influenced by the char-

v

acter of oriental societies but also deeply affected by the impact of the West. Its main concern, however, is with recent events and present conditions as ingredients in an acutely problematic social situation.

Asia, indeed, is on the move, and this in more than one sense. Where his grandfather knew little of the world beyond the horizon, the oriental peasant today feels himself pushed and pulled by the demands of trade, by political ambitions, by subtle changes in his own desires and fears. Often he has a sense of belonging to a world community, even when its nature is to him still obscure. Still deeply attached to the home of his fathers with its accustomed way of life, he is aware that other folk, too, have their particular traditions, are to be respected for their loyalty to ideals somewhat different from his own, and indeed may have something to contribute to his enjoyment of life, his peace of mind.

The war has driven many thousands back to barren hillsides and to jungles dripping with tropical rain, has brought larger numbers into new contacts with other civilizations. Conscripted, pressed into labor gangs, sent far away to help re-establish industries in some distant place or to gain food from strange soils, these peasants will return with new learnings—some good, some bad, according to their luck and to their own simple appraisals. Thousands of them will have become foot-loose and adventurous. They have seen where a living is to be made other than by backbreaking toil on exhausted fields that should long have been given back to nature's restoring care. They will have become attracted by the ease with which an engine or even an improved hand-tool enables a man to do his daily chore. There is no more popular cause in the East, and especially among the younger people, than the demand for better implements, no prestige more eagerly sought than that of the man who knows how to operate a machine.

One must visualize these personal experiences, these new impressions, and the changes forced on men's thoughts and habits, if one would understand the meaning of the statistics and statistical estimates which, as the following pages will show, come to us from the Orient with such bewildering abundance—and sometimes also with bewildering contradictions. If we wish to know the meaning of all those figures we must constantly keep in mind that they represent men and women and children with feelings much like our own, though brought up differently as to self-expression and self-restraint. Curves forecasting population trends are hazardous enough in our own society where we are somewhat familiar with the influences that shape them; they are of dubious authenticity when the same techniques of prediction are applied to oriental societies—unless those who use them are equally thorough in the study of the concrete realities for which the statistical symbols stand in an alien world. Special caution is required also because census enumerations, registration of births and deaths, and other demographic reporting are naturally less complete and less reliable in pre-industrial societies than they are in our own. Nor are the explanations given in the original sources or their translations always adequate to save the Western interpreter from errors additional to those for which his own lack of precision or acumen may be to blame. (So much in advance apology for inaccuracies which scholarly minds may discover in the present study, and in the hope that the reader will take single statements of fact, especially statistical ones, less seriously than the statements of general trends which they are intended to illustrate.)

Our main purpose has to do neither with the past nor with the distressful present but with the future. All the governments in eastern Asia and all the governments with interests there will, when the war ends, have their own population policies. If international co-operation for the future security of the region is to have practical results, it must attempt an integration of these policies in a single regional—and eventually a single world—policy.

With the return of peace the new mobility in tradition-bound Eastern societies will become amenable to international manipulation. Even during the progress of the war and in the period of growing tension which preceded it, not all the shifts of population in eastern Asia were automatic responses to pressures; some of the most important, as we shall see, were directed movements for specific social or strategic ends. The difference will be that henceforth such manipulation and such planning will be in the interest of peace and progress. The United Nations are pledged, not only each in respect to its own nationals and subjects, but also jointly as guardians of the world community, to place the welfare of the native people everywhere before any other aim.

Relief of population pressure through a redistribution of population, through more intensive uses of available resources, and through influences brought to bear on the differential growth of populations, are related tasks. In every case, the human reality must be considered along with more abstract political and economic factors if the remedies sought are to be sound. Some hundreds of thousands, perhaps millions, of Asiatics need no other help than permission to return home as best they can. Others, finding their homes destroyed or their modest farms impaired, will need assistance to tide them over until their fields again yield a sufficient living. Yet others may have to be repatriated with government aid and under government supervision. Further millions, partially rooted in a new environment and with no worth-while source of livelihood to return to, may have to be encouraged to settle permanently where they find themselves: they will enrich lands which in the past, lacking the application of human labor and ingenuity, have contributed all too little to the wealth of humanity.

As in Europe so in Asia, too, there will be groups that cannot, or do not wish to, return to their former habitat because, whether through their own fault or not, their relations with other ethnic groups there have become so bitterly hostile as to permit of no friendly commerce between them for a long time to come.

Some groups, or the more enterprising members of many groups, may wish to take part in great projects of resettlement, entailing further journeying, even though their success may by no means be sure. Some of these are as individualistic as most pioneers, but others desire to serve an impersonal cause: the building up of new centers of industry, the taming of a wilderness, the reclamation of lands once fruitful but blighted by war or civil strife.

The interchange of populations between countries and continents sets even greater tasks for modern statesmanship. Originally the present study was limited to eastern Asia, but for the sake of realism it was found necessary to discuss also the prospects of Asiatic emigration outside the region. National laws the world over have closed the opportunity of immigration and settlement to Orientals. On the basis of these laws, economic conditions have grown up which, in some instances, would be adversely affected by a sudden change in basic policies now. In other instances this controversial question can safely be reopened because it is now possible, as it was not in the past, to regulate all immigration, oriental and occidental, in such a way as not to undermine established labor and living standards. And in all instances it is possible so to modify restrictive immigration laws as to save the self-respect of any race or nation. It was only through a heedless disregard of the feelings of men with little political power in the first place that protective measures deemed necessary by reasonable people assumed the character of intolerant and unjustifiable discrimination against Asiatics.

In short, while the author does not feel called upon to present a program to solve all the major population problems of eastern Asia, he considers the time opportune for their examination. It is possible to foresee some of the more troublesome elements in the situation which we shall confront at the time peace is concluded. Agreement may be reached at least on the direction in which solutions must be sought. Preliminary measures can and should now be devised to prevent much unnecessary hardship and maladjustment when no more bombs fall from the sky and the great homeward trek begins. Looking beyond such immediate tasks, one may wonder whether the outside world can do anything really effective to see to it that rational policies are applied to the drift and growth of Asiatic populations, or whether the painful processes which throughout history have kept down numbers will repeat themselves, whether the stronger and culturally more primitive stocks will to the end of time subject the weaker ones or drive them into the sea. Elsewhere, on stages not quite as large, human intelligence has learned at least to mitigate if not altogether to avert the tragic consequences of our animal instincts. Perhaps, under the shadow of our worst man-made catastrophe, we shall have the will to apply what little we possess of science and good sense to the source of our greatest future threat. There are six hundred million people in eastern Asia. And we can no longer hope to dominate them by force.

This study, begun privately, was completed under the auspices, first, of the International Secretariat, then of the American Council, of the Institute of Pacific Relations. It owes much to the advice of the international research staff and to that of several American scholars who have been good enough to read and comment upon a mimeographed draft which was circulated under the same title as the present volume. The text has been greatly changed since that circulation, and the author fears that one or other of his friendly critics may be embarrassed by having his name associated with this publication. He therefore extends to all of them a heart-felt anonymous thanks. And it is to be understood that the author holds himself alone responsible for all statements of fact and opinion not directly quoted from other sources. In doing so, he would like to mention, however, that this general survey would not have been possible without the specialized studies in this general field of interest previously initiated and brought to completion by the Institute of Pacific Relations and quoted in the text.

CONTENTS

xi

PART IV

POSTWAR PROSPECTS

PART V

EMIGRATION BEYOND ASIA

PART VI

CONCLUSIONS

ASIA ON THE MOVE

PART I

LAND AND POPULATION

1

MAIN CURRENTS OF MIGRATION

RURAL POPULATIONS with only cart tracks between villages, and sometimes not even these, tend to be traditional in culture, conservative, difficult to move. It is this, and not some mystic element in the oriental character, that makes habits and institutions appear less changeable in eastern Asia than they are in regions technically more advanced. The forces of attraction and propulsion have to be stronger to effect population movements of like strength.

There are also other basic differences which should be kept in mind—differences not so much between East and West as between peoples in different stages of civilization. Americans are prone to think of an excessive growth of population in areas with a land use that is already high as the main cause of migration. The peopling of North America had its main source in an overflow of population from regions with intensive land uses. Such a centrifugal flow from areas rich in natural resources across the seas, and from our own Atlantic Coast into the virgin forests and prairies of the continent, occurred only, however, during a particular phase of our Western civilization—the era of expansion, roughly from the fifteenth century to the end of the nineteenth. There are examples of it in Asia, too: the Russian settlement of Siberia and the recurrent expansion of China beyond the Great Wall and, to a lesser extent, into the unattractive wilderness of

1

the southwestern borderlands. But this kind of migration by pioneers is secondary to a historically much more prevalent population movement which occurs both in primitive and in highly advanced stages of civilization.

Movements of population from the margins inward rather than out from centers of population characterize both primitive agrarian and modern industrial migrations. Even those migratory movements which at first glance may seem examples of a population overflow into less densely populated areas often prove, on closer examination, to be motivated by the attraction of new concentrations of capital and, hence, of opportunity.

For example, between the seventh century and the middle of the nineteenth there have been several periods of Chinese expansion, each of them corresponding to a growth in political strength. In every case migration followed trade, and colonies composed of southern Chinese groups speaking the same dialect formed on many coasts and islands of the Asiatic tropics. But none of them assumed the magnitude of large-scale colonization. It required a combination of circumstances which did not occur until the second half of the nineteenth century to give that population flow the proportions of a relief of population pressure in the densely occupied coastal lowlands of the southern provinces. The plantation industries of the Western Hemisphere had, with the abolition of slavery, lost their cheap labor supply; the steamship had lowered the cost of long-distance transportation; effective European control had been achieved over the rich virgin lands of Farther India and Malaysia. Chinese mass migration to the south started, not at a time of exceptional population pressure, but on the contrary at a time when a succession of famines and rebellions had reduced the population by many millions. What set the coolie emigration going as a mighty stream was not a new burst of desperation in a land-hungry peasantry but fresh fields of opportunity created by foreign enterprise and capital.[1]

Large-scale emigration from northern China to Manchuria may serve as another historical example. Although Chinese infil-

[1] Ta Chen, *Chinese Migrations with Special Reference to Labor Conditions,* Bulletin 340, U. S. Bureau of Labor Statistics, Washington, D. C., 1923, pp. 4-6.

2

tration started many centuries ago, it was incident to conquest and trade, "colonial" in the European sense rather than in search of land. As Owen Lattimore observes, the Chinese never has shown a longing for the wilderness and is reluctant to move beyond the reach of the civilization he knows.[2] Large-scale migration to Manchuria followed toward the end of the nineteenth century the construction of railways and wharves, the opening of mines, and the beginning of heavy industry, also the systematic production of such crops as soy beans for exportation. Labor recruitment in North China opened the sluice, as it were, to a flood of seasonal labor migration which soon rose so high as to necessitate stimulation only in exceptional years. As living conditions worsened below the Great Wall with the fall of the Manchu dynasty and a series of natural calamities, the seasonal ebb and flow of labor changed into a steady movement of peasants from Shantung and Hopei to Manchuria for permanent settlement. But although this movement assumed the characteristics of mass pioneering it could not have taken place without the large previous investments in communications and in industry. The central stream, even in the years of greatest diffusion, was toward areas already well settled, not to the uncultivated fringe.[3]

These two examples from China illustrate a more general trend.

The colonial movement still continues to some extent as a means of settlement for those crowded out of the homeland, but at its height it was the result of particular circumstances which are gradually disappearing from the world. Its prime cause in Europe was the failure of modern science to give the poor that share in an enlarged production at home which, when applied to means of travel and of transportation, it afforded in the more individualistic economies of the distant virgin lands. The typical European emigrant to the "New World" took advantage of the combination between free land and his ability to market his product in competition with that grown nearer the large

[2] *Manchuria, Cradle of Conflict*, New York, 1932, p. 9. See also p. 117 *et al.*

[3] C. Walter Young, "Chinese Colonization and the Development of Manchuria." *Problems of the Pacific, 1929*, Chicago, 1930, pp. 423-65.

centers of population. With the rising tendency of land values in America, and with the increasing grip of monopolistic organizations on the previously free enterprise of the pioneer, the fact that cultivable land is still available has ceased to be the main attraction. In so far as he is not propelled by poverty or oppression but attracted by the hope of a better life, the European emigrant feels the call of industrial and commercial rather than that of agricultural opportunity.

The main currents of migration in our time flow towards and not away from thickly-populated areas. Migrants are drawn by the magnetism of economic opportunity, which today is found in the cores of industrial life, in the towns and cities and their environs rather than in the open spaces of overseas or colonial lands.[4]

The part now played by industrial and commercial opportunity was always in primitive and agrarian societies played by soil fertility and other natural advantages. Just as in our modern industrial society, so in the older agrarian one, the contrasts of opportunity for livelihood are not absolute but relative. Where with the existing state of culture the reproduction of population remains below, or on a par with, the reproduction of the used portions of the natural wealth—game, forest products, pasture, fish, and other—the impetus to invade richer settled regions does not, usually, arise. But when the growth of population exceeds the reproduction of resources, an overflow to some known or rumored promised land of plenty is more likely to take place. This also happens, of course, when the resources have diminished—either from natural causes or through overuse—even though the population may be stationary, or when life has become less secure through human encroachments—such as slave raids or military conquest. In short, movements of population from the margins to the centers of natural wealth rather than from the centers of population to the unsettled and less fertile margins characterize the long history of agrarian civilizations.

Still thinking in terms of "European expansion," many Western writers visualize eastern Asia as a sort of marginal space at the edge of our world community, to be more fully peopled either by the extension of that community or by affording every

[4] W. D. Forsyth, *The Myth of Open Spaces*, Melbourne, 1942, p. 3.

4

facility to the growth of oriental populations. They fail to realize that the same causes that have tended to stop or to slow the centrifugal population movements in the West also operate in the East, although there a different set of social and political conditions may somewhat hide the main currents of human migration. Instead of equalizing population density, the migrations of recent times there, too, have intensified inequalities. The most primitive and the most modern motivations combine to accentuate a centripetal flow. From the highlands and mountain slopes where small remnants of more primitive peoples still lead their rude and insecure lives, there is a slow drain to the lowlands, reinforced by military and labor recruitment. From upland villages the centers of intensified commercial agriculture draw some of their labor forces. But all this is a mere trickle compared with the human tides that have laid out plantations of many square miles and dug deep mines, converted marshes into flourishing rice lands, and burst the bounds of great cities.

In former times, dispossesed groups have sometimes been driven from their homelands literally into the sea; in recent times they have more often been driven beyond the seas to supply cheap labor for large-scale enterprise. The Occident's colonial expansion in its later phases meant for the Orient a distortion of ancient economies under the mastery of foreign trade. Under its compulsion, the self-sufficient seclusion of agrarian societies was disrupted. It substituted new for old forms of exploitation, new machine equipment for old tools, and so in some instances accentuated the differences in the value of various kinds of land and in others reversed them. By drawing seaward most of the commercial product it added new geographical diversifications in land value to those created by new land uses.

The new communities planted by foreign trade, equipped with facilities for modern living, themselves became lodestars of desire. From the undeveloped hinterlands came the poor in search of work and the rich in search of new sensations—sometimes also of new security and a genuine enhancement of personal worth. Railroads were constructed, coastal and inland navigation was organized, to serve the new needs, to "get at" the minerals and the lumber and to "get out," by new channels, the few tons of surplus product or commercial output which any one com-

5

munity might have to add to the baled and crated shiploads destined to feed the industries of distant lands. These arteries of communication helped to promote a centrifugal migration to the extent to which new economic activities in the hinterland exceeded the potentialities of available labor supply. But they were far more instrumental in the stimulation of a centripetal movement of population, draining population away from the interior and adding to the density along the coastal belts.

Great river valleys in China and Burma are known as "rice bowls." That is a good, illustrative phrase. Such a bowl, sometimes of immense fertility, attracts the hungry from the less favored areas around. There may be a constant slow influx of new population, and there may be invasion with use of force. The lowland people tend to be less sturdy than the invading highland hordes, and handicapped by immobile property; so their defense eventually breaks down. There are then not only more mouths to feed, so that individual land holdings get smaller, but impoverished and oppressed classes form. Thus a centrifugal migration of the landless takes place, who must seek their sustenance elsewhere. Those actually driven out may be members of the former dominant ethnic majority, or they may be groups that were marginal before, minorities that now lose their hold on what few resources they had before.[5] The population groups in South China that have made the largest contributions to the emigrant stream originally had their habitat farther west and either had been attracted to the more fertile coastal belt or had been driven there by one or other of the expansionist Sinification campaigns that started early in Chinese history and were conducted with great savageness under Ming and Manchu emperors. The emigration from northeastern China,

[5] For example, there is a hint in John E. Embree's study of a Japanese community that those who in former times were recruited for contract labor in Hawaii were not members of average households but representative, rather, of families which themselves were newcomers to the Japanese village where they lived. (*Suye Mura, a Japanese Village*, Chicago, 1939). This fact also seems to be borne out by the measurements which Harry L. Shapiro and Frederick S. Hulse have made of Japanese migrants and their descendants in Hawaii and continental United States. (F. S. Hulse, "Physical Types among the Japanese," *Studies in the Anthropology of Oceania and Asia*, Cambridge, Mass., 1943, p. 124.)

on the other hand, may be said to be the end result of a constant worsening of conditions in China Proper after the Manchu conquest. As far as is known, the migrants from Shantung, Hopei, and Honan are not members of oppressed ethnic minorities; they seem, rather, to be representative of the average impoverished peasantry of North China. Similarly, Korean emigration to Manchuria in recent times did not result from a natural excess of births over deaths and consequent land hunger, but from a conquest-created impairment of livelihood, of which we shall have more to say below (p. 93).

The characteristic picture for eastern Asia, then, is a predominantly centripetal population movement, creating reservoirs of population on the most fertile land; and these spill over from time to time in expansionist, centrifugal movements. This process is aided by weakness of government and civil war, which, again, are partly explainable by conquest and insufficient development of internal communications. The marked differences in density of population in all parts of eastern Asia do not reflect alone corresponding differences in the value of the resources they offer; they reflect general differences in economic opportunity—a term which includes stability, relative freedom from oppression, and tolerable agricultural relations.

2

CAUSES AND IMPEDIMENTS OF MOBILITY

China

TAKE CHINA, for example. Here about three-fourths of the population are concentrated on one-seventh of the total land surface, that is, in five areas: the central section of the northern plain, the Yangtze delta, the coastal belt south from the Yangtze, the central or Hupeh basin, and the "red basin" of Szechwan. There are, in addition, a number of lesser concentrations in other parts of China. Always the population is dense in river valleys and thin in the uplands. Why? The Chinese farmer prefers intensive arable production on plains and in valleys to upland cultivation. He is sometimes charged with being ignorant of the pastural arts, overgregarious, and therefore disdainful of the opportunities of animal husbandry when this involves residence in homesteads rather than villages.

But in many parts of China there has been a retreat from the uplands simply because life and property have not been safe. This is true not only of mountainous areas but also of elevations, by no means high, that surround the lesser valleys. Remnants of upland villages which at one time were much larger may be seen in areas as distant from each other as Shansi and Anhwei and Fukien. Even where dangers of civil war and banditry were no longer imminent, there was in recent times often so oppressive and rapacious a type of local government that movable property could not be protected against repetitious heavy "taxation." And this recent condition is merely a recurring phase of weakness in an economic system which alternates between strong centralized governments that must take their taxes in the form of the less perishable products (grain rather than livestock), and predatory provincial and local governments that appropriate anything they can lay their hands on.[1] In such a system, the only animal husbandry that can prosper intermittently is that which may be carried on in intimate connection with the arable-farm household.

While internal disorder and the resulting insecurity have in every period of a weakened central government been important factors in the distribution of China's population, it should not be forgotten that this very weakness, during the latter part of the Manchu regime and during the first thirty years of the Republic, was at least in part the outcome of outside interference with that country's internal affairs. The effect of a foreign trade supported by military force has already been referred to in general terms. In China, the concentration of that trade and of the primary industrial processes connected with it not only drained wealth and labor power from the older centers of pro-

[1] For a brief discussion of this phenomenon see Karl August Wittfogel's introduction to *Industrial Capital and Chinese Peasants*, by Chen Han-seng (Shanghai and New York, 1939), p. x.

8

duction—both rural and urban—but also cut into the older channels of internal trade.[2] These had never been deep, wide, or long but, apart from maintaining the imperial granaries and store houses, had mainly served a convenient local and regional specialization within narrow limits. But they had helped to hold together the loose fabric of the empire, and their disruption greatly weakened the national government. Moreover, the dominance of foreign interests kept the Manchus in power for half a century longer than their regime would have lasted under the traditional system.[3]

Support of the national government in its efforts to overcome inner dissension had begun, in the early 'thirties, to induce the Western powers to relax their excessive control of the Chinese economy, more especially to enable the government through currency stabilization and a more diversified tariff to regain its mastery over internal markets. But there had not yet been time for a real recovery from the injuries inflicted by many decades of foreign interference when once more Japanese imperialism raised its head. Whatever may have been the combination of motives for the invasion of Manchuria in 1931, there can be no question that the military aggression of 1937 had for its primary purpose to prevent a further consolidation of that economic and political strength which was then being forged in Nanking.

The whole period is one of unusual interest to the historian, and especially to the historian of population movements. Civil strife and banditry, always in China symptoms of a weakened central government, had not only led to the abandonment of much upland farming, but had even diminished the cultivated area in some of the densely populated counties of the south-eastern provinces. Towns and villages were fortified, outlying fields were left idle, and the sea in some places poured through the neglected dykes. Wealthy landlords and merchants who had been in the habit of conducting a profitable loan business in grain from local stores found it safer to ship their harvest stores to some defended town. Some left their families in the villages

[2] Ch'ao-ting Chi, *Key Economic Areas in Chinese History.* Chicago, 1936, p. 150.

[3] E. R. Hughes, *The Invasion of China by the Western World,* New York, 1938, p. 30.

while they spent most of their time to conduct business in the town. Others, attracted by the speculative profits of a trade less bound to the crops of one locality, moved to the large cities. As the drift to the cities increased, it carried along many of the artisans and the managers of incipient industries. As always, the exodus of wealth was followed by an exodus of talent.[4]

Vital statistics for China unfortunately are too incomplete to permit of reliable deductions as to the influence of this urbanization on birth-rates. Any comparison of urban and rural birth-rates would be vitiated by the fact that, contrary to experience in the Occident, families are largest in the "upper class," [5] and that the proportion of prosperous families is probably largest in the port cities. In Manila and Singapore, the birth-rate of Chinese residents is lower than that of the natives and might falsely be attributed to their longer habituation to urban life, were it not for the more obvious explanation that women are disproportionately few in the immigrant Chinese population.[6]

The low tariff forced upon China, the strife between contending war lords, banditry (unpaid soldiers and landless peasants), the attractions of city life, and the concentration of capital prevented that spread of economic modernization which in the Western world we identify with the term Industrial Revolution. China could not follow European or American examples in gradually converting her many local crafts into full-fledged modern industries, capable of feeding many mouths. With an estimated average population density of probably about 250 persons per square mile—not much more than that of several European countries still regarded as mainly agricultural—China has come close to the limits of saturation for a purely agrarian society.

[4] For a case study of this exodus, its causes and consequences, see Chen Han-seng, *Landlord and Peasant in China*, New York, 1936.

[5] C. M. Chiao, Warren S. Thompson, and D. T. Chen, *An Experiment in the Registration of Vital Statistics in China*. Oxford, Ohio, 1938, p. 46.

[6] In an earlier study, Chi-ming Chiao came to the conclusion that China's exceptionally high birth-rate is explained with the high proportion of women of marriageable age who are married: the fertility rate, while much higher than for any European country, is actually lower than that for Japanese married women. (*A Study of the Chinese Population*, Milbank Memorial Fund, New York, 1934, pp. 41-2.)

Those limits, of course, are elastic. Even a modest investment of capital in the reclamation of marginal lands, and of lands neglected but not naturally marginal, in the building up of consumer industries, and above all in internal communications, would at least for a time enable China to support its present population on a much higher plane of comfort than it has enjoyed in recent decades.

In the long run, every improvement in land uses, a more advanced technique of food production, and industrialization may, of course, produce so great a decline in death-rates as to negate all these benefits. Social changes are slower than technical ones, so that a higher production instead of raising the plane of living would be absorbed in the maturing of larger families.[7] So pessimistic a forecast, however, is based on the assumption that the change of social attitudes must be "left to nature," whereas in reality it can be speeded by appropriate measures.

In any case, it is difficult to separate the influence of industrialization from others. In several European countries and in North America, many instances can be found of a modernization in living standards, with concomitant changes in social attitudes, that cannot entirely be attributed to the introduction of new industries or to the mechanization of traditional crafts and agricultural processes. They also result from increased communication: improvement of roads, introduction of motor vehicles and steam vessels, greatly increased circulation of reading matter, radio, new educational services, and so forth—all contributing to a more cosmopolitan outlook and more refined habits without an actual urbanization of residence or important change in occupations. In oriental rural societies, such modernization has not been observed because the influences named, though they occur here and there, are as yet too weak to counter the familial core of the mores. Some students of population problems foresee that every relief of population pressure through improvement of social conditions of such densely populated countries as China, India, Java, or Tonkin which does not derive from a process of industrialization will be short-lived because with a continuing

[7] See Robert W. Barnett, ed., *Factors in Chinese Economic Reconstruction*, Institute of Pacific Relations, New York, 1942, p. 3; and J. Lossing Buck, *Land Utilization in China*, Chicago, 1937, pp. 369-71.

high birth-rate the pressure on the resources will soon again take up the slack. This view is justified by an examination of the existing facts and trends. But to conclude that the Chinese social outlook can be changed only through industrialization attributes to that process of mystic quality which it does not possess. To say that the Chinese birth-rate cannot be reduced except by means of revolution in China's basic economy is to disregard the moral of a well-known Chinese story—that of the Roast Pig.

Internal migration and resettlement will play an important role in the postwar economic reconstruction of China. They will also provide opportunities for that socialization of outlook without which an annual addition of some five million to the population would soon absorb every benefit from social improvements. Governmental measures to redistribute population will necessarily at first be directed toward the solution of urgent immediate problems. But they need not be blindly oblivious of the danger. There are, indeed, many recent evidences that China's statesmen are greatly concerned with this question of population growth. It is only too evident that man-power alone affords no military security while widespread poverty impedes every military effort. Therefore, China's postwar plans of industrialization call not only for the building of centers of heavy industry but also for the building of an industrial society with the skills, habits, and living standards pertinent to continuous high-class production. And the plans for the development of transportation also are designed not merely to assist in the marketing of commodities traditionally produced in different parts of the country and thus to raise prosperity, but also to modernize the social life of the Chinese countryside.[8] Only when the immediate crisis is passed, when the inflation of the currency has been mastered and an adequate revenue has been assured to finance the necessary foreign purchases and to attract foreign capital, will it be possible to proceed energetically with those educational and other social measures that are essential if an early stabilization of the population is to be achieved.

In the meantime, development of road and river transportation, river conservancy, irrigation, and reforestation are the prin-

[8] See Guenther Stein, "Chungking Considers the Future," *Far Eastern Survey*, XI, 18, pp. 190-3.

cipal means of bringing more land into use. Decentralization in China does not necessarily mean a trek over long distances, a profuse exodus to the Far West, at least not in the first stages; but rather a reclamation, at relatively small cost, of arable land that has gone out of use and of uplands not far from present areas of dense population. Square miles of former rice land in Kwangtung are covered with salty marshes; whole counties in Shantung are inundated by preventable floods; valleys in Shansi are strewn by uncontrolled spring floods which leave wastes of stony debris as far as the eye can see. Erosion has created sandy deserts in Hopei, Honan, and Anhwei where once were rich, irrigated fields.

Lack of transportation has held back the natural mobility of the people. It has reduced their defenses against banditry and warlordism. Mobility is a prerequisite for any program that may be undertaken to level out the worst anomalies of population density in relation to resources. The Chinese laborer and peasant must be able to "get away from it all" if his lot is ever to be improved. And this is especially so in those areas where absentee landlordism and despotic local rule keep them in subjection.

Southeast Asia

IN ALL the rice-growing countries the distribution of population is very uneven. Thailand, for example, is probably underpopulated if we accept any of the current definitions of optimum population; [9] but the central alluvial plain, together with smaller valley and coastal areas, contain the bulk of the population.[10] Carle C. Zimmerman some years ago drew attention to the interesting fact that the areas with densest population are also those with the highest degree of mobility.[11] His investigation showed that of every 100 families in the central crowded section,

[9] See, for example, E. F. Penrose, *Population Theories and Their Application*, Stanford University, 1934, Chapters II and III.

[10] Virginia Thompson, *Thailand: the New Siam*, New York, 1941, pp. 323 ff.

[11] *Siam-Rural Economic Survey, 1931*, Bangkok, 1931, p. 17. For other interesting facts on the causes and results of Thailand's uneven distribution of population, see the same author's "Some Phases of Land Utilization in Siam," *Geographical Review*, 27 (1927), 378-93.

76 had children residing away from home. The corresponding proportion for the northern section was 47, for the south 64, and for the northwest 54. These figures are astonishingly high, anyhow, even though they include children working at the same occupation as their parents (usually agriculture) in the same or a neighboring village. But they derive significance from the fact that a high degree of mobility in Thailand is correlated with educational facilities and ability to read and write. Professor Zimmerman also sees significance in the fact that more boys than girls had left home, contrary to the trend in Western countries.

In Burma there is a similar concentration in the lowlands thrown out into the sea by the Irrawaddy River. Here an alluvial and coastal area with high natural population increase—probably by more than 75 per cent since 1900—is fringed by zones of colonization with reclamation of tidal jungles for paddy and of uplands for rubber and other plantations. Indian and Chinese immigrant settlements contribute only about 4 per cent of the total population the overwhelming majority of which in the lowlands is native Burmans.[12]

The density of population for Burma as a whole is one of the lowest in eastern Asia, 72 per square mile, but varies greatly, as may be expected, with the diversity of soils and climates. In Pegu (including the lower Sittang Valley) it is 215, in Irrawaddy (with the delta of that river) 198, Sagaing 46, and the Eastern (Shan) States 28. The vital statistics also appear to be influenced by the great differences in environmental conditions, though registration is by no means complete. J. Russell Andrus, American economic authority on Burma, considers both the birth-rate and the death-rate reported in 1939 for the registration areas too low: they are 35.3 and 25.1 respectively. In the poorer agricultural districts, where the soil is poor but the climate relatively dry, there are proportionally fewer births but also fewer deaths than in the environs of Rangoon.

On the Malay Peninsula, the greater part of the population is

[12] Arthur Geddes, "The Population of India: Variability of Change as a Regional Demographic Index," *Geographical Review*, XXXII, 4 (October, 1942), 572.

spread along the western coastal belt.[13] Here it was mainly colonial economic policy rather than differences in natural advantages for native agriculture that made for a very uneven distribution of population; or one may say that ease of communication—natural harbors, rivers that go far into the interior—and not natural fertility determined the concentration of labor-absorbing enterprises on the western and southern rather than the eastern coast of the peninsula. Karl J. Pelzer observes that this concentration did not, in fact, begin with large-scale commercial agriculture but with tin mining, and that the clearance of land for plantations largely followed roads that had been cut through the jungle with the ever-growing appetite of the authorities for tin as the main source of public revenue. Most of the plantation crops are developed from forest plants and flourish on forest soil.[14]

In the Philippines, population density ranges from 9.5 per square mile on the island of Palawan to 539.9 on that of Cebu.[15] In some provinces of Cebu and the Ilocos, however, even though there is little urban concentration, the densities are three and four times as high as in Cebu as a whole. According to Karl J. Pelzer,

Most of the people in the Philippines cultivate small farms rather intensively and are, on the whole, crowded onto plains and into valleys, while extensive areas of hinterland lowlands, uplands, or mountain country—remain either thinly settled or empty. . . . Although more than half of the land in the Philippines is considered cultivable, only 13.3 per cent of the total area was actually under crops in 1938, with 22.4 per cent of the total belonging to farms.[16]

In the Netherlands Indies, small densely settled areas are widely distributed over the islands; but only Java, with an

[13] C. A. Vlieland, in "The Population of the Malay Peninsula—a Study in Human Migration," *Geographical Review*, 24 (1934), 61-78, gives an interesting account of the demographic factors that account for the uneven distribution of Malaya. Incidentally this case study shows how difficult it is to anticipate the effect which large-scale immigration will have on population growth even when all pertinent social factors are taken into account.

[14] *Die Arbeiterwanderungen in Südostasien*, Hamburg, 1935, pp. 62-3.

[15] *Census of the Philippines*, 1939, II, 42.

[16] *Pioneering in the Asiatic Tropics*, New York, *in press*, Chap. IV.

average of 809 persons per square mile, can be said to be over-populated.[17] The lowest density here encountered in any of the residencies is that of Bantam, West Java—332 persons per square mile, the highest that of Soerabaja—1,382 persons per square mile. Taking only the cultivated land, the respective densities are 980 and 1,951, with 1,370 for Java as a whole. Indeed, there are few other agricultural areas—and none that is not under wet rice cultivation—to rival the crowding of people to be found in some parts of Java. The explanation is the fertility of a soil constantly refreshed with the deposition of volcanic ashes by a multitude of mountain streams. Java belongs to those countries which, according to Dr. Warren S. Thompson's classification,[18] have so little margin for agricultural expansion and also so little prospect of an early industrialization [19] that neither the birth-rate nor the death-rate has come "under reasonably secure control," and this despite the government's efficient health services and welfare-centered economic policies. As long as the birth-rate "still approaches the physiological maximum," there can be no lasting remedy for recurring waves of poverty and disease.[20] The great differences in population density cannot be equalized when almost everything possible has already been done to utilize for productive purposes the natural wealth distributed unequally over the island. There is, however, this ray of hope, that Java itself is part of a dependency which extends over many other islands, some of them—and among them the largest—by no means yet on the verge of overpopulation.

The colonization of Javanese on the Outer Islands began in 1905 with a settlement project in the Lampong Residency of South Sumatra, involving some 25,000 acres and about 30,000

[17] The population densities of the larger Outer Islands are: Sumatra 44.5 persons per square mile, Borneo 10.2, Celebes 57.3, New Guinea less than 1. With 7 per cent of the land area, Java has 70 per cent of the population of the Indies.

[18] *Plenty of People*, Lancaster, 1944, p. 94 *et seq.*

[19] In 1930 only about 6 per cent of the Javanese population lived in cities with a population of more than 24,000; and even of this small proportion many still owned and worked on land.

[20] In 1815, Java had a population of only about five million; by 1890 this had grown to over twenty-three million, and by 1940 to almost fifty million, with an annual increase of about 600,000.

persons. Many thousands of Javanese also took up land in Sumatra without aid from the government. They were former plantation workers who continued to offer their services at harvest time when the large enterprises usually were short of labor. That their lot was better than in the home community appears from the fact that they drew many of their relatives and countrymen after them. Between 1905 and 1932, 47,000 Javanese colonists settled in Sumatra; in the one year 1938, 35,000 came, and in 1940 more than 50,000.[21] The economic depression of the late 'twenties and early 'thirties was, of course, the main cause both of the spontaneous and of the government-promoted migration. This now extended also to other parts of Sumatra and to Borneo and Celebes. With the breaking down of the earlier inhibitions to home-leaving, and the more automatic recruiting of settlers through the letters and home visits of settlers, the government was able to rely more on individual enterprise and to reduce the cost of its own participation in the movement.

Indo-China offers an especially striking illustration of the fact that not geographical situation but configuration determines the distribution of population. Only the two great river basins, that of Tonkin and that of Cochin-China, are densely settled. Thirteen per cent of the total land area of Indo-China contains 78 per cent of the population.[22]

Migration in all these countries, as now politically constituted, is of course part of a movement that knows national boundaries

[21] Wibo Peckema, "Colonization of Javanese in the Outer Provinces of the Netherlands East Indies," *Journal of the Royal Geographical Society*, CI, 4 (April, 1943), 145-53.

[22] The population density of Tonkin, 195.6 persons per square mile, is slightly greater than that of France. The delta area has a density in many places exceeding 1,250—compared with an average density of only 10 for Laos and 44 for Cambodia. A recent study of the International Labor Office accounts for this inequality with the recentness and sparseness of means of communication in the interior, the inability of the different population groups to get on well with each other, the attachment of the largest of them —the Annamites—to their homes, and of course differences in climate and fertility. (*Labour Conditions in Indo-China*. Studies and Reports Series, B 26, Geneva, 1938, pp. 7-8.) For a full discussion of this unusually interesting situation see Pierre Gourou, *L'Utilisation du Sol en Indochine Française*, Paris, 1939 (shortly to be published in English translation).

only in modern times. It has been induced throughout history by the urge of hunger: the pressure of nomadic highland people upon sedentary lowland people. Occasionally this movement has been reversed by sea-borne invasion and, in recent times, by a managed labor immigration that has driven native farmers inland and upland. A small but interesting example of this is the pressure of coastal Malays in Borneo upon the more primitive Dyaks of the interior.

Pressures and Dislocations

MUCH OF WHAT has been said about lack of mobility as a cause of excessive concentration in China also applies to other parts of eastern Asia. The scope of spontaneous migration is much more restricted than it is in the Occident. Until recently, there were few usable roads, for example, out of the overcrowded Ilocos coastal provinces over the mountains into the much less densely populated and yet agriculturally favorable northeastern provinces of Luzon. Like the Japanese, the Filipinos have certain cultural characteristics that are explainable with the former lack of communication—other than hostile—between small population groups that are closed off from the interior of their valley homes by mountains and have only the sea for their outlet.

Scattered areas of dense population throughout the East Indian Archipelago, and probably others, too, result from piratical incursions and foreign conquest. Piracy forced the people on these fertile coasts to move their homes close together. This made, as in China, for a tradition of gregarious living and intensive land uses. Now, when an area has a highly developed agriculture and a large population, it becomes very attractive to any aggressive nation with superior military power. Such populations are easy to tax and easy to rule. However, we have to distinguish between the effects on population of two kinds of conquest. In central Java, western Malaya, and also, perhaps, Tonkin, colonization by the invaders has profited from concentrations of population that were already large. On these wet lands a thick settlement was wealth. Wherever you have a class structure based on conquest, you are likely to find the peasant bound to the soil by a number of devices; emigration is made a crime, the local ruler and his ancestors are deified, respect for the lares and penates—or what corresponds to them in the native theology —becomes the predominant creed.

But occidental invaders came to eastern Asia with a different purpose. They came to carry away the products of Asiatic lands, not to enjoy them on the spot. And they had to defend their monopolies against armed competitors. Both for business and strategic reasons, therefore, they often created their own new centers of activity, collecting centers, factories—in the older meaning of the word. As a result, we see today concentrated populations in and around such parasitic urban growths as those of Manila, Singapore, Hong Kong, Shanghai, and Dairen. In time, such ports became centers of industry; the traders found that by entering manufacture they could add to the profits from transporting raw materials in one direction and finished goods in the other. These industries in the coastal cities attracted others from the interior and so distorted far inland both the established patterns of trade and the distribution of the population.

This second type of foreign influence on internal migration has become by far the more important in recent times. In China, as we have seen, population movements not only have been set going by the growth of the port cities, but also have followed the building of railways, with foreign capital, inland and to the frontiers. Similar influences have been at work elsewhere. The large foreign-controlled cities have by their enterprise attracted labor; but they have also, by the conveniences for good living and profitable speculation which they afford, encouraged absentee landlordism and thus intensified the social maladjustments of village life through which large numbers of peasants become landless and foot-loose. Another effect has been their destructive influence on village industries, often an essential part of the peasant's livelihood. In this respect, the large cities of Japan rank with the urbanizations caused in other Asiatic countries by foreign influences. Of the population increase between 1931 and 1935, 20 per cent was absorbed by Tokyo Prefecture alone, 16 per cent by Osaka, and 24 per cent by the five other urban prefectures. That is, the large cities of Japan together account for three out of every five additions to the population in those five years.[23] Although these proportions can be paralleled in other industrial countries, this is remarkable since in Japan large-scale industry has been far less destructive of the small workshop and home industry.

In the Philippines, urbanization is characterized by elements more nearly akin with those in southern China. It started, as already mentioned, with a need for protection against pirates and against feuds. This made for close settlement and a tradition of gregarious living. The Spanish rulers and the Church subsequently fostered this tradition for purposes of better control. But in more recent times the social stratification of Philippine society, made possible by that control, has been the principal cause of further urbanization. Absentee landlordism and the close connection established between wealth and political power have made Manila the Mecca of every Filipino who wants to be somebody.[24]

Improved communications in the Philippines and in Japan favor urbanization but have not yet reached the point—except between Kobe and Osaka, where the topography produced a drawn-out urban district—at which the advantages of industrial decentralization create a sprawling urban district.[25]

In summary, modern enterprise in eastern Asia, by creating new centers of population, has in many instances broken up the previous economic coherence within and between both thinly and densely populated areas. It has made the population more mobile both for internal migration and for emigration. The effects of Shanghai, for example, can easily be traced on some old and formerly prosperous seats of industry in Chekiang which, by the greater advantages of the foreign-controlled port city, have been robbed of both their capital and their more talented and enterprising townsmen. Similarly, in northern China you may see

[23] Teijiro Uyeda, *The Growth of Population and Occupational Changes in Japan, 1920-1935*. Tokyo and New York, 1936, p. 7. For the more recent urban growth see below, p. 51.

[24] Cornelio C. Cruz, "Population and Land Utilization in the Philippines." *Problems of the Pacific*, 1933, New York, 1934, p. 386.

[25] In British Malaya, too, although one would hardly think of the peninsula as urbanized, almost one-fourth of the people, 23.2 per cent, live in cities of more than 10,000 inhabitants. The corresponding proportion for Netherlands India is 7.5 per cent.

small towns where promising recent growths of industrial specialization have been ruined by the competition of Tientsin and Tsingtao. In Japan, the recruitment of workers in the villages for temporary urban employment has held back the industrial development of the countryside without creating a compensating psychological urbanization and class consciousness among the workers.

It is important to understand these various forces and effects because too many people imagine that all will be well for the hard-pressed populations of eastern Asia, once the danger of military aggression has been removed. These few illustrations may also help to remind us that planned resettlement will not be the principal task of social reconstruction, important as it may be in certain circumstances. The disproportions between natural resources and density of population, with their distressing concomitants in depressed living conditions, will be eliminated more surely if barriers are removed and the natural enterprise of simple people is allowed to flow toward those opportunities which they can recognize.

PART II

WAR AND INTERNAL MIGRATION

INTRODUCTION

IN THE EARLY 'THIRTIES, international migration in eastern Asia was to a large extent arrested and even reversed in its course. This was one of the results of the general trade congestion which stopped the wheels of industry and crammed the godowns (warehouses) with unsalable commodities. The world heard of the new immigration restrictions, of the repatriation of contract laborers, and other international aspects of the human situation; but actually the shifts of population *within* some of the countries of eastern Asia, as a result of falling exports, have been even greater.

Filipinos were repatriated from the United States, and thousands more left on their own account. But in the crowded villages of the Ilocos the fact that few of them could hope for re-employment on the sugar and pineapple plantations of Hawaii was more serious. Netherlands India alone of the colonial countries recognized in the disastrous fall of prices for its export commodities a challenge to its whole economic system that must be met by something more than temporary expedients. It entered upon a vigorous campaign to encourage subsistence farming and village industries to correct a central weakness. That weakness exists in all advanced colonial systems which are safe only as long as they can find outside markets for their products and have nothing to take the place of the natives' meager share in the returns from foreign enterprise when that enterprise stops. Connected with

23

the more fundamental re-orientation in the Indies were plans for internal resettlement as a relief of overpopulation.

In the present study we are concerned not only with the effect on population of the prewar world economic depression but with the combined effects of that event and of the subsequent southward expansion of the Japanese empire and the war itself. A certain amount of historic reconstruction is necessary for an understanding of the situation which the United Nations will confront in eastern Asia on the victorious conclusion of their campaign of reoccupation. The military operations, preceded in China by a ten-year period of Japanese political pressure, wrought a destruction that cannot be measured only in ravaged fields and burned homes. Families were broken up, whole communities were dispersed. Disease and famine accompanied them in their flight. Large numbers lost both their possessions and their means of livelihood.

To the suffering of individuals must be added the effects of war on the delicately balanced structure of Asiatic societies— the embodiment often of a high form of pre-industrial civilization. Over an area larger than North America that structure has retained its hold, has been recognized by modern governments as the surest guarantee of law and order. But its authority was impaired in many places by the withdrawal of hereditary rulers, leading families, or elected persons in whom it was traditionally vested. It was impaired also by a conquest which often took no account of established sources of authority but substituted for them others by elevating obscure and "co-operative" individuals to a rank in no way sanctioned by public opinion. Most of the legitimate governments were in exile or seated at distant temporary capitals. Their provincial and local organs in some instances simply disintegrated. In such circumstances the Oriental naturally turns to those near by whose age or social status gives them prestige or who possess some special ability, such as literacy, to give weight to their words. But such local men often are unfit to carry social responsibility just when the normal bonds of the community are loosened and when there is a crying need for leadership. Cut off from his usual sources of authority, the Asiatic refugee thus found himself spiritually and morally homeless; and this, too, made for a disorderly drift of population where a

24

guided and socially less harmful retreat might have been possible under other circumstances.

In modern oriental society there is a latent conflict between tradition-minded age and adventurous youth—youth that has some glimmer of the larger world and feels attracted by it.[26] At a time of social commotion this tension is accentuated: thousands of young people who in another day would have taken care of their families now wandered off to look out for themselves. Often this was, in fact, the only way in which they could escape military or labor conscription.

In short, the population movements in eastern Asia which concern us in this study spring from several causes. Some started a long time ago and had, as we shall see, their impetus in abnormal local or regional conditions. Some are continuations of drifts that go back to former centuries. Some have been set going in recent years by acute want, the cause of which can be traced to a disrupted world trade. Some are in the nature of evacuation. And some represent a re-infiltration of refugees into their former homelands even before their re-occupation by the lawful governments. In some instances, the war and enemy requisitions accentuated movements set afoot some years earlier by the world economic depression. In others, the plans made by governments for the relief of population pressure were disrupted when war came, and a disorderly flight took the place of programs of resettlement already under way.

3

SOUTHEAST ASIA

PREPARATIONS FOR DEFENSE and then the war itself interrupted the planned redistribution of population in Netherlands India— a shift primarily motivated by considerations of native welfare and not by those of commerce. Similar plans, but less advanced

[26] Bruno Lasker, *Peoples of Southeast Asia*, New York, 1944, Chapter X.

and less thoroughly conceived, were formed in the Philippines. The Japanese menace, internal group conflict, and inadequacies of the administrative machinery interfered with a more rapid execution of even the more advanced parts of such plans. President Quezon and his advisers were well aware, as were the Netherlands Indian officials, that merely to take a few thousand families out of a densely populated area and plant them somewhere else does not permanently relieve population pressure unless it is accompanied by other measures. In both countries, but especially in the Philippines, the great need is for far-reaching reforms in agricultural relations, so that the sending areas will not nullify the effects of the relief by continuing to create a landless proletariat without opportunities of employment. Neither country has, as a matter of fact, had time to start a resettlement project of numerical importance. But the experiments which they have set going have been carefully studied and in the decade after the peace will be followed by resettlement schemes of more epic proportions.[1]

What effects the war itself has had on internal migration in the countries of Southeast Asia, it is too soon to see. We have read of the destruction of certain towns and cities. But war swept over the greater part of that region with such giant steps that relatively little destruction of physical property took place, compared with that in China. Of the 150 million or so in Southeast Asia the great majority are peasants and live in lightly built huts which are easily replaced, provided bamboo, thatching material, perhaps nails and hinges, and above all tools are available. Even the loss of a harvest, however serious it may be for the household or the village afflicted, is not in this region of abundant crops as catastrophic a blow as it would be almost anywhere in the Temperate Zone. The more primitive native peoples and those semi-nomadic groups that move every few years to cultivate a new area of cleared forest land may not have been disturbed in large numbers.[2] Local government in Japanese-occupied terri-

[1] Some of these resettlement schemes are described and examined in detail by Karl J. Pelzer, in *Pioneering in the Asiatic Tropics*, New York, *in press*.

[2] Guerrilla warfare in Java, Celebes, and perhaps other islands of the Netherlands Indies, continued until the latter part of 1942 but does not

tory seems to be functioning; it functions better, probably, in the dependencies with indirect rule—the greater parts of British Malaya, North Borneo, and Netherlands India—than in those where European officials have for so long held almost autocratic powers. Whether the Japanese Army Command, where it has effective control, is more concerned in loot or in the maintenance of order, we are not informed. In either case, while some farming communities may have retired into the mountains or into the jungle to lead a more primitive existence as free men, it is improbable that the immediate effect of the occupation on population has been very great. There can have been little change in the accustomed routine in the densely populated areas devoted to native farming. Large requisitioning will have made life more difficult but is no novelty; memories of similar events survive in every part of Asia. Small numbers of patriots or nationalists here and there continue to engage in guerrilla warfare as their mode of life until the enemy is dislodged; there can hardly be many of them.

In Indo-China, as we have seen (p. 17), a serious problem of overpopulation has for long existed in the Tonkin Delta. The French government policy to facilitate the resettlement of Tonkin peasants in Cochin China has been continued under the Japanese occupation and, according to authorities on this area, may have to be intensified, as part of the postwar relief operations.[3] It would in a sense be repatriation, since the excessive population of Tonkin is a result, largely, of a former government-sponsored migration to the delta area from Cochin China and Cambodia.

The occupation and the war in China also have had the effect of stopping many of the industries in Haiphong and Hanoi.

seem to have involved the dislocation of any substantial groups. However, many native village communities took to the hills as their only possible protection against the seizure of their women and their property by Japanese looters. A high Netherlands official reported from Australia in October, 1944, that more than half a million Javanese had fled from their homes to escape compulsory enlistment in military construction works.

[3] Admiral Decoux, the French administrator under Japanese control, has been credited with a plan to transfer a million rice farmers from northern Tonkin to southern Annam. As far as is known, less than a thousand families had been resettled under this plan by June, 1943.

27

These cities were close enough to the Chinese border for a successful flight of large numbers, especially perhaps of Chinese urban minorities, from Japanese oppression into Chinese territory. In the early days of the occupation there was a considerable crossing of the border also of patriotic Annamites from further down the coast who were trained in Kwangsi for guerrilla fighting against the Japanese.[4]

Other effects of the occupation on population movements in Indo-China are difficult to estimate. It is probable that in the provinces of Laos and Cambodia, partly awarded by Japan to Thailand, there have resided considerable numbers of Annamese, Tonkinese, and persons of Chinese blood who will have attempted to reach a community of their fellowmen remaining under the old administration. The Annamese, according to a census estimate of 1936 (there has been no census since 1921), with 16,700,000 persons, make up about two-thirds of the total population. Their economy normally requires exports not only to Japan but also to China and the Philippines, to the former two counties not only of rice but also of industrial raw materials; and any fall in exports seriously impairs their plane of living. According to such reports as are available, there has been some shift from rice production to that of fiber crops; but an unknown proportion of the people have adopted a more primitive and self-sufficient living since imported goods were unobtainable. The plight of those accustomed to consume manufactured goods has been increased by the deterioration of industrial plants in Indo-China itself and that of rolling stock; this class includes especially the city populations of Tonkin, which have been reported by refugees to be near starvation even though there were abundant rice crops in the Upper Delta. This situation, and not an alleged danger from air raids, sufficiently explains the desire of the government to transplant as large a part of the unemployed population as possible to the South.

Similar effects of the war on populations in other parts of Southeast Asia are gradually becoming evident. Vast amounts of agricultural products are reported to be accumulating or rotting in the fields. Not only export markets have gone, but many home

[4] H. G. Quaritch Wales, "The 'Co-Prosperity Sphere' is Getting Restless," *Free World*, VII, 6 (June, 1944), 548.

markets too, because means of transportation are lacking. Thus, for example, the people of northern Burma are starving; and parts of British Malaya and of India are in serious difficulties because they depended for food on part of the Burmese rice surplus of some three million tons a year.

The Burmans normally rely on the export of rice for a large part of their livelihood. India and Ceylon used to take almost two-thirds of Burma's rice exports, the countries occupied by Japan barely one-seventh. Shortage of ships deprived Burma of most of even their market and prevented a making up for this loss by increased shipments to Japan.[5] As a result, the war has brought about a great reduction of rice cultivation in Burma. According to one recent estimate, about one-half of the acreage lay fallow. The shortage of shipping was only one cause of this; another was the inability of the Japanese, here as in Indo-China, to find anything to offer in exchange for the desired foodstuff except a worthless currency. This latter circumstance accounts for the failure of the Japanese to take advantage of the Burmans' plight by inducing them to produce cotton. Although there has been a large increase in the area devoted to that crop, it neither came up to Japanese expectations nor compensated the Burmese for their loss of normal trade.

Some relief in an otherwise unbearable economic situation was afforded by the flight of perhaps half a million Indians. This not only relieved the labor market but was utilized by the Japanese for a generous gesture to attract Burmans to their cause: the legal claims to ownership of land and mortgages on the part of absent Chettyars were simply abolished, and Burman farmers who had barely been able to make a living now found themselves restored as owners, with the additional compensation for their loss of markets that they did not need to pay their land tax for 1942, and probably not that for 1943 either. In lower Burma, according to J. R. Andrus, this may affect the cultivators of some 50 or 60 per cent of the land.

[5] In peace time, Japan was not an important consumer of Burmese rice. When crops failed in Japan Proper, Korea, or Formosa—the main areas of supply—Central China, Indo-China, and Thailand were able to make up the deficiency. The maximum rice import from Burma in any one year was a quarter of a million tons, and that was exceptional.

Whether the Burman population really appreciated this generosity at the expense of the Indians may be doubted, as there are many reports of their stubborn resistance to the attempts of the Japanese to recruit them for labor required in connection with the military campaign. Apparently, the gifts and attractions offered them for labor services did not suffice to seduce them from their homes and fields; and the recruitment of labor has assumed more and more coercive forms. Even so, the military authorities were obliged to introduce Indian laborers from Malaya where their man power was not as greatly needed as behind the front in Burma.

In neighboring Thailand, the war situation as regards disposal of the rice surplus in war time was less acute. An economist familiar with that country explains this as follows:

A bad flood in October 1942 brought widespread destruction to Thailand's 1942-43 rice crop, reducing the harvest by one-half or more and reducing the rice planting for the following season to perhaps two-thirds of normal. Moreover, because of the war situation, any rice imported into Malaya now comes from Thailand and not from Burma, transported either by rail or by sea through the relatively sheltered Gulf of Thailand.

The effort made by the Thai government, at the behest of Japan, to persuade farmers to grow cotton, jute, and other industrial products in place of rice, would, according to the same authority, have been a less effective influence on the rice surplus even if the farmers had responded more fully than they actually did.

Malaya suffers from a food shortage by no means fully relieved by a compulsory mobilization of Chinese laborers to grow food. Some of the strenuous efforts made by the Japanese authorities to bring Malaya closer to self-sufficiency in food may, however, be expected to have lasting and beneficial results: Japanese agricultural experts were brought in to advise Chinese and Malay farmers; Formosan rice seeds were introduced in the hope that with their use it might be possible to secure two rice crops a year; new lands have been opened up for rice cultivation by Chinese farmers; and a number of Chinese farm settlements have been established.

The native people seem to have been little disturbed by the

invasion. But with the removal of some thousands of Malays and
Chinese from Singapore to Johore, there to raise food products,
the Japanese overlords incidentally broke an old-established
taboo against Chinese participation in the growing of rice on the
peninsula. While this movement was for the purpose of relieving
unemployment in the city, the Japanese took another step apparently for the purpose of assuring themselves of an adequate
labor supply: they prohibited the movement of population from
one Malay state to another. This means that in the more densely
populated sections they closed an avenue of escape for those
whom they wished to force into labor services.

In the Philippines, the three million or so persons usually engaged in sugar production, as laborers or sharecroppers, were
most seriously affected by the invasion. The Japanese did not
realize their ambition to convert a million Philippine acres to the
planting of cotton, but it is known that cotton production in 1943
was sufficiently advanced to permit a Japanese hope that by 1944
the Islands would be self-sufficient in clothing materials. Although some land previously under tobacco and other crops also
was included, most of this extension of fiber-growing must have
been on sugar plantations, probably with a considerable reduction in year-around employment for those normally dependent
for their livelihood on the sugar centrals. Many of the sugar
centrals were dismantled, with the aim of reducing sugar production by two-fifths, while coconut oil and cordage factories
were maintained at their full strength.

More serious a source of dislocation of people was the destruction of homes, of crops, of shops and factories, and of
shipping craft during the hostilities. Rural homes are easily re-
built in the Philippines, where materials are still available, but
the damage of bombing attacks on cities and towns was serious
enough to force evacuations because of the ensuing unemployment of population groups usually engaged in trade, transportation, manufacture, and a multitude of crafts. The gold mines
were flooded by retreating American forces and do not seem to
have resumed operations. Some of their equipment, in fact, was
dismantled for use elsewhere. There is also the demobilized
remnant of the Philippine Army. Some of the ex-soldiers were
employed, under Y.M.C.A. direction, to peddle small commodi-

ties—one of the methods introduced by the enemy to control and ration the retail trade, which was placed in the hands of neighborhood associations so as to cut out the Chinese middlemen.

In the Netherlands Indies the Japanese invasion meant a recurrence, in an aggravated form, of the serious economic situation created a decade earlier by the closing of world markets for the dependency's principal export commodities. About one-fourth of the cultivated area was devoted to export crops, and these constituted about two-thirds of the total exports (in value). For millions of Indonesians the great plantations represented an essential if not the only source of income. The loss of export trade other than to Japan, therefore, meant unemployment for those wholly dependent on wage labor, including many of the contract workers employed on the Outer Islands and a large part of the city populations, and loss of cash income for the even larger numbers of peasants whose land holdings are insufficient to support them.[6] Fortunately, the more densely populated sections of the Indies, and especially Java, are well provided with roads and road vehicles, so that a return of urban workers to the villages and a dispersion of villagers to marginal lands permitting of a somewhat meager and primitive livelihood was possible. For their own purposes, the Japanese used native labor to repair roads, bridges, and railroads damaged during the campaign. Migration is hindered, on the other hand, by the disrepair of rolling stock and especially by the destruction of a large proportion of the vessels on which inter-island communication depends. Even with the full use of shipyards and the establishment of new ones, the loss of shipping is the most serious hindrance to relief through planned redistribution of population. Resort to forced labor on the part of the Japanese authorities when labor for defense works and Japanese export industries did not volun-

[6] Plantation work in Java did not, of course, cease but has had to be manned by forced labor so ill recompensed as to throw additional burdens on the neighboring village communities. In July, 1942, 1,100 plantations were subjected to a corporation controlled directly by the Japanese military, with the aim of increasing as rapidly as possible the supply of rubber, cotton, quinine, cacao, fibers, and foodstuffs. Evidently, this system of production under military orders did not work any too well; for, in May, 1944, the management of the plantations was entrusted to twenty-two Japanese private corporations.

tarily come forth in adequate volume, was, as already mentioned, another cause of dispersion.

There are districts where a large part of the younger men have disappeared, nobody knows whereto, and where only old men and young lads are left. In some islands the entire population has fled from the Japanese. They have left their villages and their property and have gone into the jungle where they try to live on whatever the forest may yield in the way of edibles.[7]

In some instances, whole village communities left their homes because, under Japanese coercion to produce unaccustomed crops and be paid for them in unaccustomed if not worthless currency, they could not make a living anyhow, or because when the crop was harvested so large a part was commandeered that what was left over did not suffice to sustain the people. One may conjecture, furthermore, that flight was the only recourse left open to simple villagers in the many instances where, by a mistaken zeal on the part of the Japanese command to suppress hostility, they were deprived of their lawful authorities and of those among them who exercised functions of leadership, and this in situations demanding difficult adjustments to unheard-of demands.

Throughout Southeast Asia the consequences of the war were worse in the cities than in the rural areas, because food stores there were more accessible to the conqueror and because there were fewer chances of emergency and substitute supplies. In some of the occupied areas this comparative disadvantage of the city dweller, deprived moreover of his usual job or custom, led to an exodus to at least the nearer agricultural areas; this assumed large proportions especially in Burma. Deficiencies in commodities other than food are even greater proportionately in most parts of the so-called Greater Co-Prosperity Sphere, and especially in the cities. But although they include textiles and medicines, they are not of the kind to induce a countryward migration. Many large-scale enterprises, especially those carried on with foreign capital and dependent on export markets, come to a standstill, with a complete loss of employment for both native

[7] A report of the Netherlands Information Bureau, Washington, D. C., March 10, 1944.

and immigrant workers. In such countries as Burma, where practically the whole retail trade was in alien hands, the occupation must have meant a stoppage of the customary village fairs and a boost to native crafts which in normal times compete against cheap imported goods.

There are no figures to indicate the extent to which foreign oriental workers—that is, chiefly Chinese, Indians, and in Malaya also Javanese—employed on estates, in mines, and in industrial plants have been returned to their homeland before escape became impossible. In the case of the Burmese Indians the flight was precipitous and tragic in its effects not only on the lives and livelihood of a deserving class of workers, but also on the future relations between Indians and Burmans. (See below, p. 62.) Large numbers, in any case, must have remained behind. Subsistence farming by such workers was started on both British and Dutch plantations, but we do not know to what extent this practice was adopted. We do not even know to what extent the Japanese may have been able to force rubber planters and others to continue operations with such working forces as they had.

Equally serious is the situation of those peasants in Southeast Asia who are in part dependent on wage labor for their living or who rent land from the large estates as sharecroppers or subcontractors, or who, as farmers on their own account, contract with the estates for the disposal of those products which, with the advice and under the guidance of the estate technicians, they grow for cash. All these groups, whether in the Philippines, in British Malaya, or elsewhere, are hard pressed in normal times. Many of them are perennially indebted to their landlords or to professional moneylenders; none of them make more than a bare living. Those who find themselves far from their homes will need free transportation and other assistance before they can become solvent again.

A certain shift of population took place from the densely populated communities near the estates and partly dependent on the estates, to areas with more primitive conditions. But this shift may not have been very large except where active warfare made life unsafe for a time. In Southeast Asia, the possibilities of removal from the exposed central plains and coastal valleys

34

into the hinterland are much smaller than in the Chinese areas of Japanese occupation. Fewer residents have connections of any kind outside their immediate neighborhood. There is little sense of national unity and mutual responsibility between the various native princes and local authorities. And the native workers seem to be less versatile and less resourceful than are the Chinese. There are also even greater language differences than there are in China; at least the area within which a given dialect is spoken tends to be smaller. In the congested cities of the region—Singapore, Saigon, Batavia, Bangkok, Rangoon, Penang, and many more—a majority of the small tradesmen and artisans are Asiatic aliens, many of them as unable to live and make a living away from the protection of their longer-established fellow countrymen as any immigrant greenhorn in the tenements of New York or Chicago. These people, unless they were evacuated *en masse*, would have nowhere to go.

The material tasks of relief and rehabilitation may be expected to be greater not only in the towns, but also along the highways and waterways than in the large agricultural areas, that is, wherever the Japanese occupation and subsequently the campaign of reoccupation will have impaired normal life and destroyed homes and means of livelihood. The greatest need, however, experienced administrators tell us, will be for the quickest possible re-establishment of order. The danger is that attempts by military authorities to re-create normal conditions will be impeded by inadequate knowledge of local law and custom. Forms of mass relief that interfere with the freedom of people, such as the concentration of returning city folk in camps, or that disregard established differences in status, may be deeply resented and stand in the way of full co-operation. Preparations, preferably under the guidance of people thoroughly familiar with regional and local conditions, and where necessary including plans for the rapid availability of essential building or other materials, therefore are deemed to be of the greatest importance. Moreover, keyed up as they are by many promises of a higher degree of self-determination, the more educated circles, especially in the cities, will expect to be given a share in the responsibility for the administration of relief operations; and such expectations cannot lightly be ignored.

35

4

CHINA

WHILE THE ECONOMIC DEPRESSION affected the countries of eastern Asia in proportion to the degree of their dependence on export trade, the war has made its deepest mark on China, the first object of Japanese aggression. No one knows how many people have actually fled from their homes since the war began, in 1937. Some say thirty million, some say forty million, some consider both figures too low, but most responsible students consider both figures too high. It is difficult to see how so many millions of people could have got very far from their homes, or what could have persuaded them to take up their residence at some distant place. Clearly, a distinction is necessary between migration for permanent resettlement and a temporary quick retreat from an arena of active warfare to some safe place not too far away for an early return.[1]

Few outsiders realize the extent to which internal migration in China has in "normal" times been a recourse of poverty-stricken and oppressed peasants. There are of course no complete reports, and no one knows how far back into the Manchu regime one has to look for the beginnings of this drift. Mallory, in describing the great drought that occurred in North China in 1920-21, says:

There was extensive migration of the people from the dry regions, in some localities whole villages moving out. The sale of women and children . . . reached such proportions that a special committee was organized for the protection of children. . . .

During famine periods large numbers of people migrate. Apparently there has never been any attempt to direct this migration in such wise that the people whose home ties have been severed will settle in a region where there is a possibility of permanently better conditions of life. . . .

[1] For a description of such re-establishment of a community in Free China, only 180 miles from its original seat, see Hubert S. Liang, "What the War Did to Kiangsi," *Asia*, XLII, 6 (June, 1942), 363-4.

As a general rule the wanderers do not get very far, and those who manage to survive eventually find their way back to the old home.[2]

The tenant farmer in most of China is insecure. When he cannot pay his rent he has no right to compensation save for permanent improvements. Land speculation and absentee ownership have in some sections, especially in the South, increased the ruthlessness of a landlordism which in older days would have been assuaged by social convention. Civil wars and banditry have drawn into the social vortex families which for many generations were prosperous and respected.

Capital flies from rural districts, where it is urgently needed, to be buried in the Concessions. Population flies with it; here and there whole villages are on the move, like animals breaking from cover as the beaters advance.[3]

Considering the distribution of famines in recent times, it can probably no longer be said that the famine areas correspond roughly with the oldest regions of Chinese habitation. Man-made disturbances have assumed an importance in the insecurity of farmers equaling that of aging soil. Millions of the foot-loose wanderers have been drawn into the cities, there to take part in a competition for jobs that has driven wages below the sustenance level. Millions have found refuge in the border regions or in foreign lands. But the majority are dispersed over the Chinese countryside. Some of them have found lodgment and become settled, some have followed rumors of better chances yet farther away, but most have after a lapse of time returned to the familiar landscape they had left behind. In Shanghai, which perhaps suffered more from unemployment than any other industrial center, the usual outward flow of workers to the smaller towns and villages in the interior in times of economic depression was arrested by the uncertainty of the political situation. Opportunity to make a living here reached its nadir in 1933-34, but the Japanese attack of the previous year had again brought home to the residents the relative advantage of the protection afforded by the International Settlement in times of trouble.

[2] Walter H. Mallory, *China: Land of Famine*, New York, 1928, p. 2.
[3] R. H. Tawney, *Land and Labor in China*, New York, 1932, p. 74.

In 1935, the Ministry of Industries made an investigation of the volume and effects of internal migration. It found that in a thousand districts in twenty-two provinces, almost two million families out of a total of forty million had gone away, and individual members had left an additional three and a half million families. In some areas—southern Shantung, western Hupeh, and northern Anhwei—more than one-half of the population had at least temporarily left their homes. More than a third of the heads of households were tenant farmers.[4]

The Japanese invasion produced in some places and aggravated in others famine conditions which, more than the military operations themselves, induced the westward flow of population. The southernmost province of Kwangtung, for example, was one of the first to suffer because the Japanese naval blockade and occupation of the port cities cut off accustomed rice supplies from Indo-China and Burma while the northern part of the province and adjoining Hunan suffered from a crop failure and unusual difficulties of transportation. In the spring of 1941, the price of rice in densely populated southern Kwangtung rose from Ch. $6 to $120 a hundred pounds. Red Cross shipments had great difficulty in reaching the affected areas; thousands died in one of the most tragic mass migrations of the whole war. More recently, in the summer of 1943, the same province again became a victim of pronounced famine conditions, cut off from sources of supply formerly relied upon and, perhaps, also because of a decreased food production as a consequence of continued Japanese exactions.

One factor in the situation is that some of the most densely populated rural areas, west of Canton, have for many years prior to the war been supported largely by remittances from emigrants resident overseas. Not only did the return of many of these just before the outbreak of the war and the influx of some 400,-000 refugees from Hong Kong increase the number of mouths to feed,[5] but some of the land in the Pearl River delta region had

---

[4] Hu Nai-tsiu, "The Problem of the Peasant Exodus in China," *Education and the Mass* (in Chinese), VIII, 3 (November 28, 1936); transl. in *Agrarian China*, Selected Source Materials, Chicago, 1938, p. 256.

[5] For descriptive accounts see *China at War*, April, 1942, and March, 1943; *United China Relief News*, August 7, 1943.

actually gone out of cultivation in the years of high earnings overseas.

In North China, the enemy pursued the policy of burning villages and destroying crops that could not be carried off, for the twofold purpose of making certain areas uninhabitable for guerrilla forces and of facilitating the conscription of peasants for work in Manchuria by first making them homeless.[6]

Another area that has especially suffered from famine in recent years is the province of Honan. Here also lacking transportation facilities were an important factor. A mass exodus took place toward the neighboring province of Shensi and assumed such proportions in the winter 1942-43 that hundreds of thousands are reported to have perished of cold and hunger. At one time, according to a United China Relief official, close to a million refugees were gathered along the one railroad line in western Honan, waiting for a chance to travel farther west.

This famine migration accentuated an exodus to the border region that had been going on for some years previously. Over 100,000 refugees have been settled in the Shensi-Kansu-Ninghsia Border Region between 1938 and 1943. In the spring of 1943, over ten thousand refugees from Honan were settled in southern and southeastern parts of that region and in Yen-an County. In the five years 1938 to 1943 the region received about one hundred thousand pioneer settlers.[7] This was in keeping with the program of the Border Region's administrative authority which, on March 1, 1940, was embodied in a law providing aid for migrants and initiating systematic settlement. Between 1938 and 1940, funds for refugee relief in the region had been made available by the national government. Of an initial Ch. $10,000, one-half was used for emergency relief and one-half for work relief. Four refugee workshops were set up, and later in the same year Ch. $100,000 was appropriated for additional workshops. In 1942, the Border Region Commission granted Ch. $300,000 for the relief of sufferers from flood. But the main aim, in an area limited in financial resources but rich in farming and grazing

[6] Michael Lindsay, "The North China Front," *Amerasia*, VIII, 7 (March 31, 1944), 102.

[7] *Sin Hua Jih Pao*, May 5, 1943. The total number of Honan famine refugees has been estimated as about nine million.

land, was to colonize refugees for self-help. Further sums were appropriated by the Regional government in subsequent years for this particular purpose: Ch. $75,000 in 1941, Ch. $3,000,000 in 1942, and Ch. $20,000,000 in 1943. This last substantial appropriation was intended mainly for agricultural loans, to purchase implements—the cost to be repaid by the settlers—and to set up a reserve loan fund. Most of the loans were for the purchase of draft oxen.

By 1942, some 330,000 acres had been added to the cultivated area of the Border Region; many of the refugees had become full owners of the land they cultivated, and some, usually after the third year of residence, owners of more than the minimum holding necessary for self-support. In three years, 1939 to 1941, some five hundred households including four thousand persons were settled in Yen-an County. In the spring of 1942, their number was augmented by 4,532 households from two adjacent counties in northern Shensi. Similar substantial population increases took place in the other areas of controlled and aided settlement. In addition, the Border Region offers opportunities for seasonal employment to migrants from the near-by impoverished provinces.

The large influx of Honan famine refugees in 1943 presented a need for regulation and limitation until additional funds could be raised for systematic colonization. A resettlement law promulgated early in 1943 enlarged the scope of benefits and extended them equally to persons of all classes, occupations, and origins. Further concessions were made to settlers reclaiming public land, even those hiring labor to do so, in the matter of government loans and in exemption for three years from the "national salvation grain tax." This tax exemption extends also to those reclaiming privately owned land. In addition the settlers are exempted for one year from compulsory labor services for grain and salt transportation and for highway repair; they are given full civic rights, including the right to free medical treatment in public hospitals.[8] These details are interesting in view of

[8] Most of the above data are from an article by Li Ping in *Sin Hua Jih Pao*, May 5, 1943. For an account of successes and failures in earlier farm settlements in western Suiyuan, see *Agrarian China*, Selected Source Materials, Chicago, 1938, pp. 46-50.

the differences of opinion which exist concerning the population-absorbing capacity of China's sparsely populated borderlands, a subject which is further discussed below (p. 90 et seq.).

Still awaiting an adequate documentation are those often well-organized evacuations that took many thousands of skilled workers and laborers from the coastal region to the interior of China. They did not assume epic proportions at any one time but continued as a steady stream whenever the military situation permitted—or stimulated—more people to take part in the westward movement. An official report of October, 1941, mentions the removal from coastal cities of 448 factories of which 254 were then operating in Szechwan, 121 in Hunan, 23 in Kwangsi, 27 in Shensi, and 23 in other interior provinces. Twelve thousand skilled workers went with the 120,000 tons of machinery set up in these establishments. But this represents only a movement of factories with government assistance and presumably no more than a part of the industrial plants of all sorts that have been obliged to find a new location.[9]

L. K. Tao, Director of the Institute of Social Research, in 1940 contrasted the outflow of population from some cities with the inflow of population into others which, because of their foreign concessions or for other reasons, offered refuge. The International Settlement of Shanghai by 1938 had received an addition of from two and a half to three million to its population. Tientsin's British and French Concessions, after the Japanese military operations there in 1937, gave asylum to 300,000. Peiping received a smaller, yet substantial, number of refugees after the battles in its vicinity. On the other hand, the numbers of persons evacuated from other cities are as follows:[10]

Locality	No. of Persons Evacuated	Proportion of Population
Tsingtao	250,000	About one-half
Nanking	700,000	About two-thirds
Hangchow	500,000	Almost whole
Soochow	300,000	Almost whole

[9] An objective account of China's industrial mobilization will be found under the title, "Wartime Economic and Social Organization in Free China," in the International Labour Review, XLVI, 6 (December, 1942), 692-715.

[10] The Chinese Year Book, 1940-41, Chungking, 1941, p. 44.

Locality	No. of Persons Evacuated	Proportion of Population
Hankow	300,000	37 per cent
Amoy	210,000	Almost whole
Canton	900,000	About three-fourths

Official Chinese plans for the economic development of Szechwan, Yunnan, Sinkiang, or other western provinces afford no guidance to the actual proportions of the resettlement that has already taken place or is under way.[11] For, these plans do not limit themselves to immediate objectives. Although a major object of industrialization in China's southwest was and will continue to be the creation of supply centers of armaments remote from the more vulnerable frontiers of China, the great attraction which this region—or at least the "Red Basin" of Szechwan—has always had is its ability to support a large army. The same surface resources of the region which enabled besieged dynasties to hold out for generations [12] can also be used to feed a thriving industry. Already the main food crops—rice, corn, beans, wheat, and many kinds of fruit—make room for extensive plantings of industrial crops such as wood-oil trees and rapeseed. A much larger variety of commercially valuable crops is feasible and may become remunerative if means are introduced for local processing and manufacture.

The region was difficult of access in the past because there was not enough inducement to develop adequate means of communication. In short, there is little doubt that it can support a large population; and most students of the subject endorse the soundness of the government's plan to promote simultaneously the three essentials of a successful development: settlement, internal and external communication, and intensification of production—both agricultural and industrial. The only question is whether political and financial circumstances at the end of the war will

[11] Ch'ao-ting Chi, op. cit., pp. 31-2.

[12] Actually, under the stress of war-time emergency there has been migration not only to the west but also, more recently, a contrary movement of refugees back to the eastern home provinces. Thus in the summer of 1942 some 17,000 Chinese who had entered the country over the land frontiers of Burma and Indo-China were aided by the government to return to their family home towns in Kwangtung and Fukien, and another 2,500 were waiting for transportation facilities to their native villages in the east.

be such as to permit as rapid a development of the region as the national government evidently hopes for.

In this connection, the pioneer projects of land reclamation and settlement carried out by the Border Region Authority, already referred to, deserve special attention. Their dimensions may not be large, but independent observers see in them a definite promise for the future. Thus one of the first newspaper correspondents permitted in 1944 by the national government to visit that region writes:

We have seen how the formerly barren north Shensi country, which previously had not recovered from the devastation and depopulation of the great Mohammedan revolt in the eighteen-sixties and many subsequent cataclysms, culminating in the civil war that preceded the Japanese attack on China, has been transformed into an area of intensive cultivation, stock breeding and handicraft industry. . . .

The reclamation of great expanses of waste land was accomplished not only by local residents but also by garrison troops who work on the land throughout the summer and train in military units throughout the winter. The soldiers are able to feed themselves without imposing any burden on the peasantry.[13]

Until Chinese development programs are much further advanced and some fairly large pioneer settlement projects have taken place and been observed for some time, it would be hazardous to predict the extent to which the more remote of China's western borderlands might become available for colonization. An American correspondent who has recently traveled in that region writes:

Discovery of new resources in Tibet and Turkistan and intensive colonization of the Mongolian grasslands could change measurably the balance of population in China and China's productive capacity.[14]

Several circumstances speak against the probability that the large westward drift of population is to be regarded as a continuing trend—unless it receives a large dose of artificial stimulation. These can here be indicated only very briefly. The first

[13] Dispatch from Yenan, China, *New York Times*, July 1, 1944, p. 6.
[14] Theodore White, "China's Postwar Plans," *Fortune*, October, 1943, p. 155.

and most obvious is that, after all, the existing installation of facilities for industrial production is almost all in the East.[15] Also in the eastern provinces are the reservoirs of unemployed and underemployed labor, of skills, experience, capital, and the greater part of the domestic market. The system of communications is most developed in the eastern provinces. Furthermore, China will continue to depend largely on foreign trade. Overseas Chinese and Chinese with overseas connections will be leaders in modernization and in the introduction of new enterprise. While special overseas settlements and even schools have been established in the Southwest, these groups will prefer to invest their capital and their talents within easy travel distance from the coast.

Neither these merchant circles nor any other private financial groups now determine the nature of China's economic reconstruction and industrialization plans; and the probability of considerable population shifts must be discussed quite apart from their interests in the matter.[16] But even if the mines and heavy industries in the western parts of China were to be developed by the government and circles close to the government, with such loans as it may be able to obtain abroad and at home, basic economic laws still are in force. These industries, to serve their purpose as pillars of the national security—both economically and strategically speaking—must be equipped with modern power

[15] For example, over one-third of all foreign investments in China in 1931 were in Shanghai alone; Shanghai and Manchuria together accounted for three-fifths. Although 100,000 tons of the productive machinery have been removed from Shanghai to the interior, nine-tenths of the modern plant facilities are still in Occupied China.

[16] Although modern techniques of production and transportation make possible shifts of population that would have been unthinkable in former times, it should never be forgotten that extraordinary differences in the density of occupation between parts of China go historically back over many centuries and would long have been evened out if there were not good natural reasons for them. Thus, Herbert Day Lamson constructed a table (Social Pathology in China, Shanghai, 1934, p. 234) showing densities varying from 157 per square mile on the southwestern tableland to 897 on the Yangtze Plain; but taking into account only cultivated area, the proportions are reversed: that of the Southwest tableland proves the most fully utilized, with 4,189 per square mile as against a density of 1,277 for the Yangtze Plain.

machinery. Therefore, opportunities for the employment of unskilled labor barely exceed the reservoirs of such labor supplies that are now on hand. Such industrial plans would hardly be able to absorb the labor now engaged in the western war industries. Or take the case of other public works. With the prevalence of seasonal unemployment and underemployment among Chinese peasants in the drier and higher sections of the country, there is rarely any difficulty in recruiting (or if necessary conscripting) locally all the labor power that is needed for road construction, the digging of irrigation ditches, and the like. Indeed, in the days before the war, stories came from China about power equipment standing idle because, with the high cost of gasoline and oil, it was more profitable for contractors to use manual labor. This would not affect the setting up of modern industrial plants in peace time; but the whole level of agricultural employment will have to be raised before such a tradition can disappear, and until it does disappear together with the semi-idleness that gives rise to it, only a revolutionary change in China's major economic policies—and incidentally in the policies of the Occident toward China—could produce opportunities for the employment of large additional numbers of unskilled laborers in China's Far West.[17]

From the prospects of China's Far West we must distinguish the probable permanent effects of the war on the distribution of population between the coastal belt and the central plains. It has long been the policy of the national government to lessen the stranglehold of the port cities on the interior by industrial decentralization and thus simultaneously to raise incomes in large rural sections that have been prevented from making direct use, through manufacture, of the raw materials they produce. In this connection, political rather than military events will, of course, be decisive.[18] It was the domination of foreign interests

[17] For a discussion of such a prospect see Owen Lattimore, "Yunan, Pivot of Southwest Asia," *Foreign Affairs*, XXI, 3 (April, 1943), 476-93.

[18] Military requirements sometimes, of course, do have a continuing effect on industrial developments. It can hardly be disputed, for example, that the great arsenal at Mukden in the days of Chang Tso-lin had a stimulating influence on Manchurian industry. On the other hand, the efforts made in the spring of 1942 by the Japanese to recruit in Shanghai skilled workers for Manchurian war plants seem to have failed. An elaborate system was set

that distorted China's economic life and therewith the distribution of its population. Only if the larger industrial development programs of the postwar era are dominated by Chinese interests will decentralization be possible. And since that development will require the aid of foreign capital, it cannot be taken for granted that the old selfish and short-sighted financial policies in relation to China's economic development will not still to some extent be in effect.

There has, moreover, in some circles been a rather unrealistic pessimism concerning the future of Shanghai and the millions of people whose livelihood depends on that city. To a lesser extent one meets with similar opinions also in regard to Tientsin. While it is true that these and other port cities owe their existence to foreign trade, they do not owe it altogether to the privileged position which their foreign residents have been able to acquire through the political weakness of China. Their functions are to some extent geographically conditioned; [19] and since China's foreign trade must continue, these cities will remain important population centers. Again, the fact that such cities are fully equipped plants of human activity must not be overlooked. After five or six years of widespread destruction in China, all this investment is not suddenly going to be chucked away but, rather, will be fully utilized and so provide a more or less automatic continuation of livelihood for large numbers. The period of transition from a foreign to a Chinese orientation of commercial and industrial policies will tend to reduce the functioning of the port cities by gradual steps as the maritime trade outlets in each case for a specific if extensive hinterland. When considerations of physical safety no longer predominate in the selection of in-

up through the co-operation of the Japanese and the Manchurian and Nanking puppet governments to recruit shipbuilders, mechanics, and other skilled workers to meet the labor shortages in Manchuria and North China; but these workers simply refused to go. Later, during the May campaign in Chekiang Province, the Japanese tried to press-gang Chinese in the International Settlement through Chinese agents. Against this the Japanese chairman of the Municipal Council protested, and the practice was abandoned. Wang Ching-wei, who had made great promises to supply skilled labor, evidently had no influence in the matter at all.

[19] See B. Lasker, "Shanghai Tomorrow," *Social Forces*, XIX, 3 (March, 1941).

46

dustrial sites, land values and other economic factors will determine the location of new enterprises and cause a certain amount of decentralization. New transportation facilities will then become effective in enlarging the range of choice. But the war itself will have done little to change the population pattern in and around these cities.

5

THE SOVIET FAR EAST—JAPAN

The Soviet Far East

INTERNAL MIGRATION in the Soviet Union also is on a scale warranting a brief separate discussion before we return to more general trends. In the old Tsarist days, it would have been more accurate to speak of the migration from European Russia to the Far East as emigration or colonization. But it is precisely because all the immense territory of the U.S.S.R. has politically, economically, and administratively been placed on a level of equality that it is no longer permissible to regard whatever migration takes place within that territory as other than internal.

This migration is planned and includes both voluntary and more or less compulsory factors. The rapid growth of the steel manufacturing center of Kuznetsk in the foothills of the Altai Mountains illustrates this point. This "super-Gary," as it has been called, originally was a small town famous as the abode in exile of the great writer Dostoevski and was chosen as the site for an experiment in pure communism by a group of Tolstoyans who later were joined by a group of Doukobors from Canada and other ideological minorities. While their settlements, some miles outside the city, were encouraged to produce grains and vegetables, the industry and the exploitation of the rich coal

47

mines of the region were manned with skilled labor drawn from European Russia under a plan virtually redistributing the whole available labor force. During the war the labor shortage became so acute that in October, 1940, the government issued a decree providing for the compulsory transfer of some stated categories of skilled workers.[1]

The transference of Red Army reservists to the Asiatic coast probably was managed in such a way that at least the appearance of inducement by promises rather than by pressure was maintained. The small movement of Jews to the Jewish Autonomous Region of Birobidzhan unquestionably was voluntary; they have remained a minority in a population of about a hundred thousand. At first engaged in a variety of traditional crafts designed to supply the region with consumer goods, the settlers were, under the second five-year plan, more and more drawn into large wood-working industries, for the mass production of furniture and skis, paralleling a similar development in other districts of Jewish colonization. Jewish land settlement for agricultural production, with a strong attempt at collectivization, had been anything but successful, though Jewish agricultural settlement of a more individualistic character has taken root. The evacuation of farm populations from southern Russia to the far interior was, in some instances, compulsory but did not extend to the strategically important Far Eastern Region.

The construction of Komsomolsk, the Soviet Union's great eastern industrial outpost, was accomplished, as was that of other cities, through the response of young men and women to a patriotic call, aided somewhat by such economic incentives as wage increases and tax exemptions. In the five years 1933 to 1939, the population of the Far Eastern Region increased by more than one-fifth; but in the latter year the urban population had trebled in comparison with that in 1926. The population of Khabarovsk rose from 52,000 to 199,000, that of Vladivostok from 108,000 to 206,000.

Agricultural settlement proceeded less rapidly, although the third five-year plan provided for a 30 per cent increase of farm acreage in the Khabarovsk and Maritime Territories. There was

[1] Eugene M. Kulischer, "Recent Migration in the Soviet Union," *American Sociological Review*, IX, 3 (June, 1944), 227.

a considerable spurt toward the end of the period when armed conflict with Japan seemed imminent, but the rural population of the two territories increased by only 17.5 per cent between 1926 and 1939; and at that time new incentives were devised to attract much larger numbers of families.[2]

Free transportation, credit facilities, relief from taxation for a number of years, and assurance of remunerative prices for his products are among the inducements held out to the would-be migrant. Some other inducements did not quite come off: the construction of homes by advance crews, smooth transportation arrangements, training of recruits for the special farming conditions they were to meet. As a result, there has been a certain amount of return migration.

The original scheme for the creation of collective farms has been modified from time to time in conformity with the labor situation. At the height of the migratory movement, additional land was allotted to the workers for cultivation in individual garden plots. Later the proportion of land used in that way was reduced with the intensification and enlargement of work on the collective farms. The area divided into individual garden plots is now less than 5 per cent of the cultivated area. The rather rapid mechanization of large-scale operations has therefore evidently not produced a corresponding excess of man power. A deliberate slowing up of the influx, expansion of the cultivated area, and a rather remarkable degree of training for skilled and mechanical jobs have taken up the slack.

A comparison of the methods used by the Russians with those used by the Japanese to encourage settlement in Japanese dependencies (see below, p. 98 et seq.) shows a similarity of certain weaknesses—but very different end results. If the Japanese settler does not succeed as a farmer, his status nevertheless remains superior to that of the subject people around him, and he can insinuate himself into some semi-parasitic position; or at least he can join with others in the formation of a land company that will employ native labor. The Russian farm settler in the Far East has to face the music but, since he occupies with his fellows a position of strategic importance for the defense of his

[2] For further details see William Mandel, *The Soviet Far East and Central Asia*, New York, 1944, Chapter IV, pp. 25-31.

country, can exert pressure on his government and get obvious inadequacies in the system remedied in as far as this is possible.

The world economic depression did not directly affect the population movements within the Soviet Union, but the Sino-Japanese War and the threat of involvement with Japan did. The settlement of the Far Eastern Region has been hastened to complete preparations for a possible war with Japan. The purpose of the whole movement largely was that of making the Far Eastern Army as independent as possible of food and other supplies by way of the Trans-Siberian Railway.

In postwar years, the colonization of the Far Eastern Region unquestionably will remain part of the Soviet Union's policy, even if the danger of Japanese aggression is altogether removed. For, that colonization has other than strategic purposes, too. One of them is to exploit the natural resources of the whole realm as economically as possible, another that of creating a new center of production for foreign trade. To quote General Yakhontoff:

> The value of the Amur Province . . . lies not only in the very fertile lands of its southern part, which is well suited for the cultivation of wheat and is rich in natural resources, but also in its position as the Russian thoroughfare to the Pacific Ocean. . . . The Maritime Province, besides abounding in minerals and timber, is also rich in fisheries and provides Russia with ports on the coast of the Pacific. Its position on the border of Korea and Manchuria, and next door to Japan Proper, solidifies its political and strategic significance.[3]

Japan

WHAT HAS BEEN the effect of the war on the internal distribution of population in Japan itself? The census figures for 1940 give some clue since they reflect the influence of the "China Incident" and of preparation for the larger military and naval campaign on the distribution of population. In the five years since 1935, with a total population growth of 5.6 per cent, the urban population had increased by 21.7 per cent and the rural population

[3] Victor A. Yakhontoff, *Russia and the Soviet Union in the Far East*, New York, 1931, p. 272. Chapter VII of this work, "The Problem of Population," also contains other pertinent data.

decreased by 2.3 per cent.[4] Still more significant, perhaps, is the difference in the growth of particular Japanese cities (even allowing, in the case of Tokyo and Osaka, for the incorporation of outlying districts which itself is a sign of population growth): Yokohama, the principal port of entry, 37.5 per cent; Nagoya, a large munitions center, 22.7 per cent; Tokyo, 15.4 per cent; Osaka, center of the cotton textile industry, 8.8 per cent; Kobe, hemmed in between hills and sea with little space for physical growth, 6.0 per cent; [5] Kyoto, the old capital and culture center, 0.8 per cent.[6] Even more conspicuous has been the growth of population in the last five-year census period of the smaller industrial centers that have drawn their labor forces from the surrounding countryside: Amagasaki (Hyogo), 154 per cent; Kawasaki (Kanagawa), 94 per cent; Kawaguchi (Saitama), 80 per cent; Muroran (Hokkaido) 65 per cent. Corresponding to these increases, the 1940 census records a decrease of population, varying from ten to twenty thousand people, in fourteen rural prefectures. Although there had long been a cityward trend of population, no previous census has shown so serious an inroad on the nation's food production.[7]

This concentration and urbanization is inevitable, not only as a general consequence of war conditions, but also as a consequence of specific Japanese conditions. Whatever the demands of war on farmers may be in other countries, Japanese strategy points to a plan to insure an adequate food supply early in the southward expansion campaign by the occupation of such rich

[4] The trend was already there in the previous five-year period. See above, p. 20.

[5] In Kobe, two of the wards experienced a substantial reduction of population through the replacement of residential streets with plants and railroad tracks which necessitated the removal of 12,000 persons.

[6] *Japan Weekly Chronicle*, April 24, 1941; *Toshi Mondai*, Pamphlet No. 41 of Tokyo Bureau of Municipal Problems, 1941. The actual population figures ascertained in the 1940 census were: Tokyo, 6,778,804; Osaka, 3,252,340; Nagoya, 1,328,084; Kyoto, 1,089,726; Yokohama, 968,091; Kobe, 967,234. Jesse F. Steiner, in "Population Trends in Japan," *American Sociological Review*, IX, 1 (February, 1944), 39, quotes on this subject a recent report of the Japanese Institute for Research of Population Problems.

[7] For other related data see *Population Index*, IX, 2 (April, 1943), 73-7; also Allan B. Cole, "Japan's Population Problems," *Pacific Affairs*, XVI, 4 (December, 1943).

food-producing countries as Indo-China and Thailand. Despite transportation difficulties which were bound to develop, it was thought that a ruthless food requisitioning in China and large inroads on the food stores of Manchuria would be easier to accomplish, in the early stages of the campaign of conquest, than a large increase of food production in Japan Proper. We are as yet without adequate data to know the extent to which these plans have miscarried. Of the existence of a serious food shortage in Japan after the first year of the world war there can be no question. The sinking of Japanese supply ships in other parts of the Pacific proceeded much faster than had been expected. It necessitated a rerouting of the available shipping that cut deeply into the planned lines of transportation across the relatively safe seas of the West Pacific. Even with the aid of native craft which brought rice, tea, sugar, and other products from many parts of the region to Singapore, Saigon, and Hong Kong, these supplies could not be transported in sufficient volume to Japan but piled up on the docks. A black market developed, and the almost prohibitive prices paid suggest that the control over existing stores is rigid and that, as a representative of the United Press was told in December, 1942, in Japan "practically no one has enough to eat."

As a colonial power, Japan has not in recent times attempted to be more than barely self-sufficient in food. The demands of farming for man power have always been considered secondary to those of industry. For example, despite all paper plans for the development of Hokkaido, the largest reservoir of unused natural resources in the Japanese Isles, the number of migrants to that island during the 'twenties and early 'thirties stayed around ten thousand a year; and, what is more, in some years the number of those who came back south exceeded the number of those who went out to take up land! Too much has been made of the climatic difficulties encountered by the Japanese farmer in the northern isle and in Karafuto. His unwillingness to adopt a mode of life very different from that to which he has been accustomed is more to the point. But the government itself did not push the settlement with great vigor. The fact is that a land settlement for extensive farming and animal husbandry in an area with shorter summers and smaller yields may be socially advantageous as part of a general population policy but is of little immediate economic value to a country with a rapidly growing population which places its main reliance on production for export. When such a country does produce food for home consumption, it does this intensively and as close to the arteries of transportation as possible, so as to keep down costs. Fishing in northern waters with dynamite and poison, yes; but a large investment of capital and man power in the development of pastures and orchards and stands of timber—all enterprises that yield but a slow return—was a luxury which an empire preparing for war could not afford.[8]

Japan's industrial population is decentralized only in the sense that the individual units of production are smaller on the average than in most industrial countries. The proportion of small shops to large plants is probably greater than in any other country with modern industrial equipment. But this does not mean geographical decentralization. Actually, increased speed of production in war time can only mean that centrally situated factories are enlarged, and that transportation delays are minimized by bringing workers to where the power and the materials are, rather than the opposite. The net effect of the war is further concentration of population also in that it tends to prolong the number of years which village people spend working in industry and thus to habituate more of them to an urban way of life.

At the end of this war, the Japanese will face three major population problems which, since no one can have advance information on the numbers likely to be involved, need here be mentioned only briefly. First, there is the further concentration and urbanization of the population commented upon just now. Even if food production should be pushed up before the war is over, this will in the long run mean an increased dependence on imported food supplies. This problem will, of course, be aggravated by the loss of those dependencies and occupied territories

[8] While a longer retrospective view of the causes that made for the distortion of Japan's population distribution is not part of the present study, the writer desires to express his agreement with Warren S. Thompson (*Plenty of People*, Lancaster, 1944, p. 104 *et seq.*) that it was incidental to basic economic changes rather than planned, and that no internal or external organization existed by which suitable adjustments could have been made.

which have supplied the greater part of Japan's food imports. Indeed, that loss will be so serious as to be the main problem. For, even if Korea and Formosa may be anxious enough to sell to Japan their surplus of rice and other food products, it will not be on terms as one-sided as was the trade between these colonies and a dominant Japan in the past. Indo-China and Thailand, likewise, may welcome the custom of Japan; but all such imports will have to be paid for with exports of manufactured goods at prices which these food producers can afford to pay. That is, a much larger part of Japan's production of consumer goods than in the past will have to be used to pay for imports instead of building up balances in foreign exchange.

The second problem is that of a distorted demographic composition of the Japanese population after the war. Adjustment to peace-time conditions will require not merely transition from the production of armaments to that of consumer goods but also a transition from the wasteful use of sweated labor to the most productive possible uses of man and woman power. In vocational terms, the great loss of life will mean that larger opportunities must be found for self-supporting women—which, incidentally, is the best guarantee against a sudden rise of the birthrate. This cannot be achieved through a conversion of heavy war industries into other heavy industries, through large public-works program, or even through agricultural development schemes. The transference from war to peace occupations can be achieved only through an industry geared to the production of consumer goods.

Third, there is the problem of demobilization and the settlement of war veterans, to whom must be added a considerable civilian population returned from the lost colonies and puppet-state protectorates. Few of the returned officials, railway workers, small business men, and *ronin* will be qualified to go on the land. And yet, despite the war losses in man power, despite the peculiar composition of the demobilized civilian hosts of imperial expansion, and despite the lack of success that has attended Japanese resettlement efforts in the past, there may be need for large-scale development projects—aided if necessary by foreign loans—to set as many as possible of the hardier unemployed to productive work. This major task of finding a peace-time economy in keeping with Japan's new position in the world does not, as we have seen, necessarily imply a need for considerable agricultural resettlement if we assume that Japan is afforded adequate freedom to purchase food and raw materials and to sell manufactured commodities in the markets of the world. But a shift from two generations' concentration on preparation for aggressive war to an era of reliance on the normal processes of peaceful commerce will necessitate some changes in the distribution of population if all the natural advantages of the country are to be realized.

In the first stage of this transformation, with the imperative need to find immediate productive work opportunities for millions of demobilized soldiers, one would expect to see planning for a combined agricultural and industrial economy in the less developed parts of the Japanese Isles to be attempted as a major resort. Opportunities for diverting into creative channels energies that have gone into trade and forced expansion exist in plenty within Japan itself. They need not be purely agricultural but may include large advances in forestry and mining and in new industries for home consumption, closely associated with the production of raw materials. But all this takes time, and so it will be necessary also to keep open avenues of external trade and to convert at least some of the war industries into centers of production for export. Nothing could be worse than a return to the typical depression economy of Japan in which the village is little more than an overburdened relief agency for industrial workers sent home unemployed, diseased, and dispirited. After five or six years of war, forced food production, and lack of artificial fertilization, the fields will not even be as capable of feeding additional mouths as they have been during previous economic depressions.

PART III

INTERNATIONAL MIGRATION

INTRODUCTION

IN THE HISTORY of eastern Asia, international migration has, as we have seen, usually been short-range migration. Only in modern times has it mastered longer distances and taken advantage of striking differences in economic opportunity. For millions of peasants, all travel beyond the hills visible on the horizon still is "foreign" migration—in the sense that, as soon as he has left the small realm dominated by his own ethnic group, the migrant is treated as a stranger and feels a stranger.

Increasingly, artificial patterns of political division—in the East as in the West—have accentuated the distinction between domestic and foreign travel. A century ago, a merchant from Amoy may have felt more at home in Manila than in Shanghai. Today he can be in no doubt as to where he is a citizen and where an alien. The earlier international migrations, if they were not connected with wars of conquest, represented intensifications of more tenuous relations previously established. Typical colonists are the soldiers left behind to guard a frontier or a newly acquired territorial possession, and the member of a merchant family left behind at a foreign trading depot to check on deliveries and to prepare shipments. But today international migration in eastern Asia has all the complications of a four-sided tournament. In the receiving country one party uses proven devices to attract the immigrant, another raises barriers to keep him out. In the country of origin, some make it their business to push sedent farmers out into the unknown—labor, as the larg-

57

est "export commodity" of southern China, has become big business—and others to hold them back. The attitude that there is something rather immoral about leaving one's village has not died out. But the numbers involved in foreign migration are still relatively small. The movements of greatest numerical importance are those of Chinese to the countries of the *Nan Yang* (the South Seas in the literal geographical sense) and to Manchuria; [1] of Koreans to Manchuria and Japan; of Japanese to Manchuria, Malaya, Netherlands India, and the Philippines; of Filipinos to the United States; of Indians to Burma and British Malaya.[2]

There have also in pre-depression years been a number of minor movements of migration in eastern Asia, most of them continuous over long periods: Indians to Thailand; Javanese to British Malaya, British Borneo, and New Caledonia; Annamites to various Pacific island groups; Filipinos to South China, Thailand, Indo-China, and Japan; Chinese to and from Hong Kong, Macao, and Formosa.

6

EMIGRATION FROM WEST AND SOUTH

REFERENCE has already been made in passing to some population groups—immigrant wage-earners in the countries and colonies of Southeast Asia—who responded to the business depression and war either by identifying themselves with the people among whom they lived and shared their attempts to escape hunger by taking up food production, or by returning to their respective homelands. It will be appropriate, therefore, to begin our brief

---

[1] Although Manchuria was and will again be a part of China, its internal administration has for so long been autonomous that, for our present purpose, it is more realistic to think of it as foreign territory.

[2] Many of the statistical data in this section are taken from Karl J. Pelzer, *Population and Land Utilization*, Part I of *Economic Survey of the Pacific Area*, New York, 1942.

survey of the war's effect on international migration with a few facts concerning international population movements in Southeast Asia just before and during the war.

Indian

STARTING IN THE WEST, it is worth recording that the Indian government in June, 1938, prohibited emigration to Malaya, nominally as a temporary expedient until the employment situation should have been improved, but actually also to put pressure on the Malayan employers of Indian contract labor. Despite the vigilance of an Indian labor commissioner and various agreements between the two governments, the conditions under which Indian laborers worked and lived on Malayan plantations were still far from satisfactory to the Indian government.

In the Malayan census of 1931, 624,000 Indians were counted, making up one-seventh of the total population. But they were one-fourth of the population in the Federated Malay States, and one-third in one of them, Selangor. Most of them had come from Madras and spoke the Tamil language. The proportion of those who have settled and are likely to become a permanent part of the Malayan population was as yet small. It was, however, growing with the increase in the number of Indian laborers who returned with their families on their own initiative after having, during an earlier stay in Malaya under contract, experienced the enjoyment of higher wages than they could earn at home.

In 1938, 215,000 Indians were employed on rubber estates (three times as many as all other nationals combined), 7,000 in mines (as against 34,000 Chinese and 6,000 others), 8,000 in factories (as against 40,000 Chinese and 3,000 others), and 48,000 in public departments (as against 11,000 Chinese and 14,000 others, *i.e.*, mainly Malays and Javanese). The imminent danger of a Japanese invasion and of food shortage gave a new impetus to Indian home migration in the spring of 1941, and this in spite of the rising demand for rubber and an almost frantic search by Malayan plantation managers for new sources of labor. How many managed to get away before the southward

59

drive of the Japanese troops will perhaps never be accurately known.

There are two forms of Indian migration to Malaya, assisted and unassisted. The latter group, composed in recent prewar years more often of voluntary labor migrants than formerly, when it was composed entirely of merchants, rose from 12 per cent of the total in 1920 to 38 per cent in 1934, 87 per cent in 1936, 89 per cent (another published statement says, probably in error, 48 per cent) in 1937, and 79 per cent in 1938. Although improvement in labor conditions may have something to do with these proportions, they reflect in the main an improvement in trade after the depression. The Controller of Labour attributes the rising proportion of unassisted migrants in the total to the desire of laborers to escape the week's quarantine imposed on those assisted by the planters.[1] Many thousands of indentured laborers were repatriated during the depression.

The Indian government also had supervisory rights over Indians employed on contract labor in Thailand and Burma. In both of these countries larger numbers of Indian immigrants were artisans and merchants. Exact statistics concerning the Indian residents in Thailand are not available. In 1934, their number was estimated as about one hundred thousand,[2] and with the growing antagonism this figure probably did not rise appreciably through fresh immigration when trade recovered.

In Burma, over a million of the country's sixteen million inhabitants spoke an Indian language. How many of these were first-generation or recent immigrants is not known. On the other

[1] Interesting details concerning labor recruiting and labor conditions will be found in the *International Labour Review*, XLII, 1 (July, 1940), 65-76; and XLIV, 1 (July, 1941), 75-6. For discerning discussions of Indian estate labor in British Malaya, see Rupert Emerson, *Malaysia, a Study in Direct and Indirect Rule*, New York, 1937, p. 31 *et seq.*; and Virginia Thompson, *Post-Mortem on Malaya*, New York, 1943, p. 122 *et seq.* The fullest recent account is that given by H. Mills in *British Rule in Eastern Asia*, Minneapolis, 1942, pp. 218-37. Mr. Mills explains the large number of unassisted migrants with a genuine improvement in working conditions. Evidence of this is to be found also in Harold Butler, *Problems of Industry in the East*, International Labor Office, Studies and Reports Series B, 26, Geneva, 1938, pp. 45-8.

[2] Virginia Thompson, *Thailand*, New York, 1941, pp. 139-40.

hand, many thousands of descendants of Indian immigrants undoubtedly are included among the ten million who, in the census returns of 1931, gave Burmese as their mother tongue. For, with the growing unpopularity of their own group, many of the second and third generation of immigrants would be likely to identify themselves with the dominant group. According to a report by a British medical officer in the Indian Civil Service, more than seven hundred thousand Indians passed through the mountain passes on foot in 1942 to regain their home country. Two hundred a day were being evacuated by plane in the spring of 1942.[3]

In 1938 and 1939, an anti-foreign agitation that had been going on for some years, led to a riot against Indian Moslems, in the course of which two hundred persons were killed and large losses of property were incurred. The Indian residents had long been disliked in Burma much for the same reason that Chinese are disliked in many parts of Southeast Asia, namely because they are sharp traders and usurers.[4]

In July, 1941, an agreement was published by the governments of India and Burma regulating and restricting the admission of Indians to Burma.

It was intended to remove from Burmans reasonable apprehension that Burma might be subjected to undue economic competition by reason of such immigration, while securing for Indians settled in Burma recognition of their proper rights. The principles underlying the agreement were that Burma had the right to determine the composition of her population, and that Indians who have wholly identified themselves with the interests of Burma should enjoy the same rights as members of her permanent population. The agreement has been strongly attacked by Indian nationalists, led by Mr. Gandhi, who urged among other points that public opinion had been inadequately consulted, and that the measure cast a slur upon Indians.[5]

[3] For details as to Indian evacuation from Burma and Malaya, see *International Labour Review*, XLVI, 6 (December, 1942), 757-8; XLVII, 2 (February, 1943), 252-3; and XLVII, 5 (May, 1943), 667-8.

[4] John L. Christian, *Modern Burma*, Berkeley, 1942, pp. 258-9.

[5] *International Review of Missions*, XXXI, 121 (January, 1942), 34. Details of the regulations may be found in the *International Labour Review*, XLV, 2 (February, 1942), 195-8. The discriminatory provisions for repatriation and penalties for what the Burmese government regards as mis-

The Indian Labour Commissioner, in an apologetic comment, realistically draws attention to the fact that Indian laborers, because of poor living conditions at home, eagerly leave their villages and their families year after year in large numbers to accept wages which Burmans accept only as a last resort and which induce in them a feeling of rebellious discontent.

Whether the agreement would have worked is now a moot question, for the Japanese campaign in Burma and grasp of its political control changed the whole situation. It is believed that about one-half of the country's Indian population, roughly half a million, escaped to their homeland, some by sea but most by land. The circumstances of the flight, wherever the responsibility may lie, were hardly such as to justify use of the term "evacuation." Most of the refugees went on foot, and no one knows how great was the death-rate among them from lack of food, exposure, and unattended disease. Not only this, but under Japanese provocation, a savage campaign of vengeance on the part of Burman farmers who had suffered from the ruthlessness of Indian moneylenders decimated the ranks of the hapless refugees, most of whom had been modest artisans and wage-earners. Not until the British Army had been withdrawn, did the Burmese Independence Army venture forth to kill as many Indians as it could. The survivors who had been unable to get across the frontier eventually sought the protection of the Japanese, which was accorded them as potential adversaries against the returning British hosts, and found shelter in the well-policed streets of Rangoon.

The Indian minority has been in Burma from the beginning of the British conquest, imported for those tasks which the Burman farmers were unwilling to do. They were regarded as physically stronger than the Burmans and certainly were more docile.[6] As a result, they formed an urban working class, and those who acquired wealth tended to invest it in loans and in land. The understandable unpopularity of the minority, when

behavior sufficiently explain Mr. Gandhi's view that the agreement is derogatory to the dignity of the Indian people.

[6] At first, many parts of India were represented among the migrants to Burma. More recently the majority came from northern Madras and southern Bengal.

increasing numbers of its members seemed to the Burmans to be parasites feeding on their own industry, increased with rising land values and losses of family holdings. More Burman farmers became foot-loose and drifted into Rangoon to compete with Indian laborers at the docks. This was the main cause of the first anti-Indian riot in 1930. But a comparison of occupations recorded for the two groups in the census report for 1931 points to the existence of competition in other occupations too. For example, 377,000 Burmans and 105,000 Indians were engaged in industry, 90,000 Burmans and 102,000 Indians in transport, 330,000 Burmans and 96,000 Indians in trade, 18,000 Burmans and 24,000 Indians in domestic service. Only in agriculture were the Burmans fourteen times as strongly represented as the Indians.

The Thailand census report for 1937 lists some 56,000 residents as of British origin, and since the number of Europeans is certainly small and there is no reason to conjecture the presence of many native Malayans, this number must be assumed to represent for the most part British Indians. Indian merchants, indeed, established commercial colonies in Siam many centuries ago, and even in recent decades few of the Indian immigrants belonged to the laboring class. Like the Chinese, they are disliked for filling the functions of a middle class which the Thai today consider themselves capable of filling. But because of their relatively small numbers, the presence of the Indians has rarely given occasion to active hostility.[7]

Arab

PASSING MENTION must be made of the Arabs as a relatively small but important element among the international migrants of eastern Asia. The Arabs have, of course, never sailed east in search of work for wages. Their immigration, what there was of it in recent years, was in the wake of old-established business and cultural connections. Historically, the Arabs have shown an ability even greater than that of the Chinese to make themselves at home among Malay peoples and to gain converts for their

[7] Virginia Thompson, *Thailand: the New Siam*, New York, 1941, pp. 137-40.

ideas and for their way of life by harmonizing their teaching with the traditions and customs of other peoples. Arab communities of some importance survive in Java and Celebes. In smaller numbers, Arab artisans, retail merchants, and money changers are to be found in port cities throughout Southeast Asia. They are among the most reputed of Islamic teachers and scholars. Most of them come from the coast of South Arabia and have no very ardent desire to return to that arid landscape.[8] The favored status which the Arabs have for centuries enjoyed in other Moslem countries is passing away, as the younger generation fails to respect their pretensions to special holiness. The bureaucracy of Netherlands India has in the past favored the Arab middleman as being more sympathetic with the native mentality than the Chinese, but has come to take a less favorable opinion of his social function as an intermediary. Among the Malay peoples, only a strong anti-European nationalist movement could possibly re-establish the Arab in his former position of recognized authority. But it is possible that a new Arab expansionist movement will develop as the present war releases political and cultural ambitions long held in check.

Javanese

JAVANESE EMIGRATION beyond the Indies is incipient rather than a full-grown movement, and is a planned extension of a well controlled movement of internal migration. Since little has been said under that heading about this movement (see above, p. 58), a few of the most pertinent facts must now be given. The population of Java has grown from about nine million a hundred years ago to more than forty million, and this chiefly as a result of the Netherlands system of indirect rule which saved lives at every turn but did nothing to wean the people from that part

[8] Some of them do: "The Hadhrami merchants have brought much wealth to their valley from the East Indies. They have brought with them not only cash, but wives and ideas as well, so that Malay is heard in many of the Hadhramaut harems, and flat-faced children play in streets and gardens." Carleton S. Coon, "Southern Arabia, a Problem for the Future," *Studies in the Anthropology of Oceania and Asia,* XX, Cambridge, 1943, p. 206.

of their cultural heritage which conduces to a high birth-rate.[9] Industrialization, frowned upon in all colonial countries as a means of absorbing surplus population, was hardly promoted at all before the recent depression, except for the improvement of household crafts and related native industries. Migration of agricultural workers to the so-called Outer Provinces—meaning chiefly Sumatra, where one-tenth of the population is Java-born—helped the development of large-scale commercial agriculture and led to a large permanent settlement of Javanese. This has been supplemented with agricultural colonization, a much slower and more costly form of diffusing population. Compared with the numbers employed on the estates in the Outer Provinces—around 200,000 in depression years, 300,000 in 1938, and a little more in the decade 1925-34—the total number of agricultural settlers was small until the middle 'thirties but is no longer negligible today, with a total of 125,000—or about one-fourth of the annual increase of Java's population—at the end of 1938. Nevertheless, the disastrous fall in the world prices for many of Netherlands India's major export products made necessary a drastic revision of the population policy. Mention has already been made of the stimulation of subsistence farming as one element in that policy. Java became self-sufficient in rice production in 1940. The building up of new export industries is another policy, including of course agricultural industries and processing operations connected with them. Internal colonization is a third. A much larger movement of assisted emigration may no longer be avoidable in postwar years. Until recently it was assumed that the Outer Provinces would be able for a long time to absorb all the surplus population of Java, and the government was hostile to any thought of planned emigration beyond the limits of the empire. This view, however, was somewhat colored by political considerations which may recede into the background. For, recent surveys in the Outer Provinces—that is, primarily Sumatra—have revealed that:

. . . the fertile land . . . is far less than might be assumed. Moreover, the land that is suitable as far as soils are concerned is not always irrig-

[9] For a detailed account of the Javanese population problem, see Karl J. Pelzer, *Pioneering in the Asiatic Tropics*, New York, *in press*, Chapter VI.

able. The Javanese farmer is used to his wet rice culture, and one of the strongest attractions of emigration is the expectation of owning irrigable rice lands. Colonization in the Indies is not a matter of individual pioneering, where settlers occupy favorable patches scattered over a wide area; it is a group effort. The area of settlement must be large enough to receive many settlers, so that the costs of colonization, public services and supervision may be reduced to a minimum. [10]

From a strictly economic standpoint, the labor opportunities for Indonesians—*i.e.*, Javanese—in British Malaya are likely to become increasingly attractive. For the present, the employment of Javanese contract workers on the estates of the peninsula is numerically unimportant; with closer co-operation between the two governments it may become more significant. The number of Indonesian residents in the British colony is not known, since in addition to those on contract many others have settled as small farmers or entered other employments. They figure among the 318,000 "other Malaysians" who make up 7.2 per cent of the population of that country. They are recruited mainly from the Kuala Lipis and Kuantan districts of Pahang, some on verbal monthly agreements, others under contractors. The indenture system was abolished in 1932. The Javenese laborers tend to mix with the local Malay population. In 1938, about 11,000 were reported as employed in Malaya on estates, in mines, and in factories. If this figure were correct one would have to conclude that a much larger number, perhaps at one time thus employed, have settled down as farmers. On the tobacco plantations of Sumatra, Javanese laborers more often work on time wages while Chinese prefer piece work, which enables them to earn more; presumably the same difference exists on the plantations of Malaya. [11]

Since the Japanese occupation, and under the partially joint administration of Malaya and Sumatra, unknown numbers of

[10] Jan O. M. Broek, *The Economic Development of the Netherlands Indies*, New York, 1942, p. 20. See also above, p. 16 *et seq.*

[11] Little is known about the more than three thousand residents of Thailand described in the census report for 1937 as Dutch. With the exception of perhaps a hundred or so, they must be assumed to be Javanese contract laborers.

Javanese contract workers are reported to have been moved from Malaya to Sumatra.

The little Javanese colonies invariably make a good impression because these subjects of Queen Wilhelmina like to surround their houses with tidy gardens, as they do at home. In fact, when given tolerable labor conditions and the chance to acquire a little land—preferably wet land for rice growing—many of them will prefer to stay. In the past, methods of labor recruiting in Java for work away from home have been ugly; but these conditions seem to have been remedied. In short, there is some prospect that Javanese settlement in Malaya will assume the proportions of a major population movement in the postwar years or as soon as mutually beneficial arrangements for exchanges of population are possible between neighbors in the western Pacific without arousing fears of political encroachment.

Javanese settlers in French New Caledonia numbered nine thousand in 1939, 15 per cent of the total population. Their treatment in the French colony under the old indenture system before 1920 was most unsatisfactory and among the Javanese themselves discouraged any further experiments in eastward migration beyond the protection of their own government. Their numbers in other Oceanic colonies today are exceedingly small, despite the fact that some of these no doubt offer better economic opportunities than do central and western Java.

Indo-Chinese

THERE HAS ALWAYS BEEN a movement of population between northern Indo-China and the neighboring countries. Indo-China itself has been settled originally by population groups moving down the river valleys from north, east, and west; but in recent times, with the growing density of population in Tonkin, Annam, and Cochin-China, it has been a source of emigration to western China and to Thailand. In the absence of adequate census reports it is difficult to estimate the volume of this emigration. Suffice it to say that the Thailand census report for 1937 lists 39,000 residents as of French origin, and the great majority of these must be Cambodians or Annamese.

From Indo-China there has also been a sponsored movement

67

of contract laborers to French possessions in the South Pacific: the New Hebrides, New Caledonia, and the less important French Establishments. The New Hebrides had just over 2,000 Indo-Chinese in 1938 (4.7 per cent of the total population), New Caledonia 3,756 (6.2 per cent); but the total number of emigrants to the islands had been much greater. Tonkinese and Annamites have been recruited for the plantations and mines of New Caledonia, less actively for the New Hebrides, since about 1902. The conditions under which these workers were employed have always been unsatisfactory. A serious scandal developed in 1927 around the employment of Tonkinese laborers in the quarries of the Société des Phosphates de l'Océanie. With the growing strength and vehement opposition of the Annamite nationalist movement, it is believed that for a long time to come there will be no organized effort to recruit Indo-Chinese labor for work in the South Pacific possessions.[12]

It has been reported that Annamese laborers have been recruited to aid in Japanese defense works on certain islands to the south. If this should prove true, these conscripts would undoubtedly wish to be repatriated at the first possible moment.

Filipino

CONCERNING FILIPINO EMIGRATION little need be said because there is so little. The population, as has already been seen (above, p. 15), is very unevenly distributed over the archipelago; but there is little inducement to move off to the surrounding countries because labor conditions in the Philippines, poor as they are, still are better than those elsewhere in that region. There has been neither much desire to emigrate, other than to the United States, nor active recruiting. In recent years, even migration to Hawaii and continental United States has been frowned upon by the Philippine government, partly from pride, partly to avoid friction, and partly because there is not really any reason why those able agricultural workers whom the American employers desire should not help to develop their own country. Systematic settlement of Mindanao, through the establishment of agricultural colonies by the government, started

[12] Virginia Thompson, *French Indo-China,* New York, 1937, pp. 163-4.

in 1913. The earlier experiments, however, proved too costly, and in 1918 the Inter-Island Migration Division was established to recruit a more suitable personnel for homesteading in selected thinly populated parts of that large island. By 1934, some six thousand pioneer families had been settled with government assistance and another thirty thousand or so had been sent under the auspices of other agencies. All this proved much too slow to accomplish the object of developing Mindanao with the aid of pioneer settlers, and in 1939 a National Land Settlement Administration was established to set up a limited number of large colonies designed on a community basis. There had not, of course, been time enough at the time of the Japanese occupation to permit of a thorough appraisal of these schemes; but some of their technical inadequacies had already become sufficiently apparent to produce plans for improvements.[13]

Smaller land settlements, on different islands, have also taken place under other, especially provincial, auspices. In addition to Mindanao, the islands of Palawan, Mindoro, Basilan, and Samar have been mentioned at times as standing to benefit from somewhat larger agricultural populations.

How many Filipinos are there in the United States? The returns of the 1940 census show that there has been no change in ten years. In 1930, we had 45,208 Filipinos in continental United States; in 1940 there were 45,563. Although the same in number, the Filipinos in the United States are less conspicuous than they were. More of them have become fully assimilated. The adult age level has gone up, and there is also a larger proportion of children. The number of young Filipinos engaged in commercial agriculture as laborers has decreased considerably.[14]

[13] For a detailed description of these projects, see Karl J. Pelzer, *Pioneering in the Asiatic Tropics,* New York, *in press,* Chapter IV.

[14] Most of the returns of Filipino residents in the United States to their home country took place on their own initiative and at their own expense during the years of economic depression. Under the law of 1933, with subsequent extensions in 1937 and 1938, which made $250,000 available for the return passage of indigent Filipino workers, not much more than two thousand have been repatriated. (The U. S. Department of Labor gave the figure as only 1,239 repatriated by 1938.) In addition, there was during the economic depression a wave of deportations by court orders which accounted for perhaps another thousand or so.

Objectively considered (which it rarely was), the number of Filipino residents in the United States never was large, in relation either to Philippine population pressure or to American labor requirements. It may be taken for granted that there will be no renewal of Filipino labor immigration to the United States, even when restrictions of a racially discriminatory character will have been removed from our immigration law. (Under the Independence Act of 1934, an annual quota of fifty Filipino immigrants to continental United States is permitted until 1946.) Employers on the Pacific Coast have become reconciled to the use of Mexican labor, the inflow of which can be better regulated in relation to cyclical and seasonal variations in demand. In Hawaii, the number of resident Filipinos dropped from about 70,000 in 1930 to 52,000 in 1940; but most of these are now permanent residents. Active labor recruiting in the Philippines stopped some years ago, and the movement of laborers between Manila and Honolulu has assumed very small proportions.[15]

The only other country where numbers of Filipino immigrants are to be seen is, curiously enough, China. They are members of Chinese-Filipino families with residences or connections in both countries. Under the pressure of increased anti-Chinese feeling in the Islands, nationalism among Chinese-Filipinos grew strongly in the early thirties. Thus, when China was invaded, and even before, thousands of Filipinos with Chinese parents or grandparents went to China to study or to engage in business. While there, they were under the protection of American consuls, until they had to leave, as subjects of the United States.

[15] The total Filipino population in Hawaii in 1940 was 52,000, as against 155,000 Japanese, 29,000 Chinese, 7,000 Koreans, in a total population of 423,000. Active labor recruiting in the Philippines for the sugar and pineapple plantations of Hawaii has in recent prewar years fallen to a low point. The general tendency, greatly increased by the war experience, is in the direction of a more varied economy, offering full employment to a permanent resident labor force; and it is possible that foreign recruiting for contract labor in Hawaii will not be resumed. The total number of Filipinos resident in Hawaii is only four-fifths of what it was ten years ago; and a much larger proportion of the Filipino community are Hawaiian-born and full citizens.

7

EMIGRATION FROM SOUTHERN CHINA

WE TURN, then, to the much larger and more complicated subject of Chinese emigration. Because of its importance it has given rise to a sizable literature, so that it is not necessary here to give very many detailed data for the prewar period.[1]

It started as an overflow. People were literally shoved off the shores into the sea. Some groups colonized such islands as Formosa and Hainan. Some, deprived of the right to own land, stayed on the water and still live by the tens of thousands on their boats.

For many generations, a stream of migrants poured uninterruptedly from the two southermost provinces of China, Kwangtung and Fukien, many of them as merchant adventurers, some to return after long voyages, some to stay abroad. They were intrenched in Malacca before the coming of the Portuguese, in the Philippines before the coming of the Spaniards, in the Indian Archipelago before the coming of the British and the Dutch. The Nan Yang, or South Seas, has remained their favorite destination.[2] There they were for centuries a master race, not coolies

[1] See, more especially, Ta Chen, *Emigrant Communities in South China,* Shanghai and New York, 1940; Kenneth P. Landon, *The Chinese in Thailand,* New York, 1941; considerable discussion also in Karl J. Pelzer, *Economic Survey of the Pacific Area,* Part I, *Population and Land Utilization,* New York, 1941; Felix M. Keesing, *The South Seas in the Modern World,* New York, 1942; John L. Christian, *Modern Burma,* Berkeley, 1942; Catherine Porter, *Crisis in the Philippines,* New York, 1942; John R. Hayden, *The Philippines,* New York, 1942.

[2] For purposes of the present study, the ethnic composition of emigrants from South China—a subject by no means as yet scientifically established—is not very important. The main distinction is between four main groups, the Punti of western Kwangtung, usually referred to as Cantonese; the Hoklo of eastern Kwangtung and southern Fukien; the Hakka of eastern Kwangtung; and the Hokkien of Fukien. All these groups have their origin elsewhere; at several periods in Chinese history rebellious population groups were driven from the mountainous interior to the coast, and colonists

sent in slave ships to unknown ports. Chinese experiences in the white man's world—North and South America, the West Indies, South Africa, Australia—have not been happy, though some who stayed through the misery of the early days grew rich. The main chapter in the history of Chinese emigration beyond the limits of Asia coincides with the worst chapter in the story of Western industrialization and imperial expansion. Soon after, the book was closed.[3]

Because of the peculiarities and differences of naturalization laws and because of much inter-marriage, it is practically impossible to say without a large margin of possible error how many Chinese are living abroad today. The number is usually estimated as between eight and twelve million. This number does not, however, include Manchuria, which is still to be regarded as a part of the Chinese Republic. The principal concentrations of Chinese population in other Asiatic countries are about 1,700,000 in British Malaya,[4] 1,233,000 in Netherlands

were introduced from distant places to pacify the indigenous population. Thus, the Hakka probably have their origin in Shantung; the Hoklo, now mainly resident in the vicinity of Swatow, came from Fukien; some of the communities or dialect groups in western Kwangtung came from Kwangsi.

The so-called Cantonese, for centuries the main carriers of Chinese trade to the countries of the south, figure less strongly in the recent labor emigration but make up a large part of the city populations, especially in Malaya. Most of the Chinese residents in Thailand are Hoklo, most of those in the Philippines Hakka. Hokkien miners are responsible for a large part of the Chinese population in the Netherlands Indies and in Malaya; the Hakka also are represented among the miners but predominate among those Chinese migrants who have taken up land to farm. The Chinese elements in the Indo-Chinese population, resulting in part from a continuous infiltration overland and in part from recent overseas labor immigration, do not permit of an ethnological unscrambling.

[3] One of the most peculiar and least-known recent episodes in the history of Chinese "coolie" emigration is the employment on contract of some ten thousand laborers from an area south of Ningpo in Chekiang to work the soapstone quarries of Italian-dominated Ethiopia. This "labor export" soon was stopped by Chinese national legislation.

[4] In British Malaya, the Chinese are a majority of the population according to the population estimate for 1941, which gives them 2,389,000 as against 2,316,000 Malays. In the Straits Settlements they outnumber the native Malays three to one, and in the Federated Malay States they also predominate. In the Unfederated Malay States, the Malays have the majority, except for Johore with its Chinese-manned mines.

GEOGRAPHICAL DISTRIBUTION OF CHINESE OVERSEAS [5]

Country or Region	Number	Year of Investigation
Indo-China	500,000	1938
Burma	400,000	
Thailand	3,000,000	
Malaya	2,358,335	1940
Sarawak	86,000	1936
British North Borneo	47,799	1931
Neth. East Indies	1,430,680	1940
Philippines	117,463	1940
Australia	12,500	1939
New Zealand	2,307	1920
Fiji	1,751	1936
Portuguese Timor	3,500	1932
India	15,000	1931
Hawaii	27,179	1930
Contin. United States	74,954	1930
Canada	42,100	1932
Brazil	158,867	1933
Central America	85,400	1933
Union of South Africa	4,500	1929
Soviet Union	250,000	1931
Western Europe	32,000	1933
Formosa	4,759,197	1933
Japan	20,050	1933
Korea	41,303	1940
Hong Kong	1,500,000	1940
Macao	435,000	
	15,405,945	

[5] *Modern Overseas Affairs*, organ of Overseas Affairs Commission of the Executive Yuan, Vol. III, No. 3. Some of the above estimates vary greatly from those given in the text which, making up a total of from eight to ten million Chinese overseas, also have at times been accepted by organs of the Chinese government. The difference is, of course, accounted for largely by the uncertainty of the national status of residents of Chinese descent in those countries where the discrepancies cannot be accounted for merely by the flow of contract labor between particular years.

India, 117,000 in the Philippine Islands (a relatively low figure which merely signifies that more of them have become absorbed in the general citizenship), 445,000 in Thailand, and 326,000 in Indo-China.[6] There are no reliable data for the Chinese population in Japan, Korea, the Soviet Far East, or Mongolia. The Chinese government from time to time publishes statistics of Chinese overseas, based on consular reports. What classes are included, or omitted from, the estimates for the various receiving countries of Chinese emigration is never made clear; but there is reason to believe that the figures for these estimates are not arrived at (nor could be) by a uniform method.[7]

The emigration from southern China has from time to time changed in character. There has been much less active recruiting by labor contractors than formerly in the last prewar decade, for example. To obtain a realistic view of the meaning of this

[6] This would seem to be an understatement unless only first-generation immigrants are included. Ta Chen, referring to an International Labor Office report, gives the more convincing estimate of about four million. In the case of Thailand, the figure named differs from another, likewise from a reputable source, by 10 per cent, both figures being for 1929, since when the Chinese colony in that country must have gone through considerable fluctuations, ending with a wild flight in 1941.

[7] *The I.L.O. Year-Book, 1939-40*, gives as the most recent figures available a total of 111,000 departures of Chinese emigrants from Hong Kong in 1938. Of these 27,000 went to the Netherlands Indies and 62,000 to the Straits Settlements. This no doubt represents the majority of emigrants from southern Kwangtung that year but may not convey information worth knowing. Emigrants often take passage to Singapore and from there continue their journey on native vessels.

For the two other major ports of emigration, Swatow and Amoy, estimates are given in the *International Labour Review*, XLV, 4 (April, 1942), based on returns of the Chinese Maritime Customs, 1940, showing a great decline in the total movement through these ports in that year as compared with the two previous years, and a small excess of arrivals over departures: 41,555 as against 40,229. The outgoing passenger traffic was relatively greatest to Thailand and Indo-China, the return traffic relatively greatest from the Netherlands Indies and the Straits Settlements. These figures, however, cannot be interpreted as indicating more favorable conditions for Chinese residents that year in Thailand and Indo-China; for it was precisely from these two countries that there was reported in 1940 an overland return migration so considerable as to induce the Chinese government to open special offices to aid the settlement of the returning migrants in five localities of southern Yunnan.

migration, in any recent prewar year, one would have had to distinguish, first of all, between labor migration (and this free or under contract) and migration in the wake of old-established business connections. But this is not possible statistically because, with the abolition of the penal sanctions of the old time labor contracts, jobs have become more interchangeable, and the person who is bound for work in a mine may wind up after a few months in his uncle's drygoods store in Palembang.

The settlements around business communities in the port cities of Southeast Asia are considerably older than the farm settlements of honorably discharged or run-away plantation laborers. Emigrants with a superior civilization do not remain hewers of wood and drawers of water. The Chinese laborer whom you see on the streets of Singapore or Manila is trying to save up for a pack of cheap trade goods and, after a few years of peddling in the villages, quite likely will establish himself in business at some crossroads, gradually shifting his emporium to better and better locations until he can establish a chain of stores or buy himself into partnership with some old-established wholesale firm. Not everyone becomes an owner of sawmills and rubber factories and banks and steamship lines, but enough of them do to call out the effort and thrift of many thousands of their fellow countrymen.

The indentured laborer in earlier years, when travel was tedious, dangerous, and expensive, often stayed away from home for many years, sometimes forever or until he felt old enough to join his ancestors. Because of their long-continued sojourn abroad, the emigrants to the United States, to Australia, or to the West Indies did not dissipate their fortunes but, when they did eventually return, were able to amaze their relatives and neighbors with the magnificence of their style of living and of their benefactions. They established the big department stores, built local railways, toll roads and bus lines, founded schools and hospitals, and gambled with princely largesse in newfangled business enterprises, apartment houses, and political careers. Among other things, they financed the Chinese Revolution.

Improved and cheapened travel, together with the growing restrictions on oriental immigration in high-wage countries, changed the character of Chinese overseas migration. Where

Chinese immigration was still permitted in the last few years before the present war, and that means principally the countries of the Nan Yang, the Chinese communities were divided into two classes: the older colonists, now increasingly identified in interest, attitude, and even language, with the country of their residence; and the newcomers who remained outsiders even when they changed their status from that of laborer or farmer to that of merchant.

The large increase in the number and size of large-scale foreign enterprises in the Asiatic tropics in the first quarter of the present century brought with it a corresponding increase in Chinese immigration, but it also set going, in times of business depression, a reverse movement, until the migrations back and forth came to resemble more the short-term labor migrations between European countries or between Mexico and the United States than the old-time Chinese migration for a period of contract labor as a first step toward permanent settlement overseas. This does not mean that contract workers do not still try to stay if conditions are favorable, but it has become more difficult for them. Their own consul sees to it that they do not hang around when out of work—on the chance that, as business improved, they might either get their job back or join some townsman in the establishment of a small business. There is more travel back and forth, and more members of the same family take part in it. There has also, in recent prewar years, been a noteworthy increase in the emigration of Chinese women—a movement now often encouraged by estate employers because it keeps their Chinese male workers happier and because it provides them with a supply of cheap and unexpectedly efficient labor if managed with a little finesse.

Corresponding to these changes, migration between Southeast Asia and southern China has become much more sensitive to fluctuations in business activity. Larger proportions of contract laborers and other emigrants return home after two or three years with little to show for their work abroad, although, while it lasted, it helped to support their families. Another result of this short-range migration experience has been a lessening of social distance between the emigrants and the stay-at-homes. Instead of arriving as "rich uncles" whose wishes must be obeyed if their benefactions to family and home community are to continue (sometimes they do get tired of their relatives and retire to a modern house in the nearest city, or even to Hong Kong or Shanghai), the returned emigrant of the new class remains "one of the boys"; and while he may not have changed much in his tastes and ideas, since he had little opportunity to get away from his Chinese labor gang, when he does dilate on the values of modern hygiene or a schooling, he is listened to with attention. Another consequence of the increased mobility is that even the older, partly assimilated Chinese colonies abroad have been brought into closer touch with the political and economic life of China.

With the beginning of the world economic depression in the late 'twenties, as in previous business depressions, the normal excess of Chinese emigration overseas over return migration was reversed. In 1930 over half a million workers were forced by the economic depression to return to their homeland, in 1931 almost three hundred thousand.[8] Anti-Chinese movements gained force in Thailand, Burma, Netherlands India, and the Philippines.[9] Thousands of independent Chinese colonists—farmers, artisans, small business men, and wage earners—bought steamship tickets home; and other thousands were repatriated under the terms of their contract. There were also many, especially descendants of mixed marriages who previously had considered themselves Chinese, who now silently disappeared into the general citizenry of their adopted country (in Thailand, more especially). The rubber people and the tin people and other large employers cheer-

[8] *Current Events Year Book, 1930-31*, Nanking, 1931, p. 141, and reports of Central Overseas Affairs Commission, Nanking.

[9] For a partial account of the legal residua of these movements in the immigration and naturalization statutes of Indo-China, Malaya, the Netherlands Indies, and the Philippines, see Norman MacKenzie, ed., *The Legal Status of Aliens in Pacific Countries*, London and New York, 1937. In the Philippines, a revised naturalization law was passed and came into effect in 1939, and a new immigration law was passed in 1940 and became effective in 1941. The effect of these two laws on Chinese immigration is described by L. Garcia in *Legal Status of Oriental Aliens in the Philippines*, Institute of Pacific Relations, New York, in manuscript. Other sources for the more recent developments are: Virginia Thompson, *Thailand, the New Siam*, New York, 1941; John L. Christian, *Modern Burma*, 1942; Kenneth P. Landon, *The Chinese in Thailand*, 1941.

fully paid the fares to get rid of their surplus labor forces, since to keep them would be far more expensive. But almost before the last boat crowded with Chinese steerage passengers had docked in Hong Hong, a labor shortage already made itself felt in Singapore. While the prospects for rubber and tin were still doubtful, in 1934, and after the Singapore immigration officials had worked overtime to enforce the most recent legal restrictions on immigration, the tide of migration turned. The following figures tell the story. After an excess of arrivals over departures of 100,000 in 1929, which shrunk to one of only 19,000 in 1930, there was a net departure of 134,000 in 1931, 128,000 in 1932, 58,000 in 1933. In 1934, arrivals of Chinese laborers in British Malaya again exceeded departures, by 41,000. This annual surplus gradually grew to 177,000 in 1937, only to fall again to 50,500 in 1938.

In the Philippines, arrivals of Chinese immigrants were in excess of departures throughout recent history. And therein, too, lies a story: Chinese do not go to the Philippines as contract laborers. Few of them are employed in competition with Filipino wage-earners. Most of the newcomers are starved-looking, ill-clad peddlers and small storekeepers. The fluctuations in net immigration here do not in the main represent changes in work opportunities for the Chinese—these opportunities vary little from year to year. They do represent fluctuations in the degree of misery in the villages from which they came, back home in China.[10]

In Indo-China, net arrivals of Chinese immigrants averaged 25,000 in the five years 1925 to 1929. From 1930 to 1934, there was an average net departure of 1,200; and this gave way to an excess of arrivals over departures of 16,000 in 1935 and 1936. The net immigration for the decade was 116,000. In 1937, the immigration seems to have been more than twice that of the previous year. Here also, the Chinese are capitalists (with a very

[10] In 1938 the Philippine Bureau of Commerce reported that in 28 provinces, not including the capital city of Manila, Chinese made up 43 per cent of the persons engaged in retail trade, as against 30 per cent of Filipinos, 9 per cent Americans, 7 per cent Japanese, 7 per cent Spaniards. Since then, the proportion of Japanese increased greatly but never reached that of Chinese merchant personnel.

small "c" as a rule) rather than horny-handed laboring men. Why they started coming in larger numbers in 1935 and kept this up in the following years is more probably explained with stages in the transference of Japan's "China Incident" to the southern shores than with anything connected with the rice exchange in Saigon. The figures, moreover, are probably not complete but relate only to sea-borne immigration. In the absence of a reliable census report for China, a computation of a total number of 326,000 Chinese, as against about 400,000 a decade earlier, must suffice.[11]

Thailand, if one may judge from unsatisfactory statistics, seems to have had an annual excess of Chinese arrivals over departures averaging 38,000 in the years 1925 to 1930, declining to one of 10,000 in the following five years. Despite the strong anti-Chinese campaign—one might even speak of a persecution with discriminatory laws—the Chinese seem to like it in Thailand; there has been an increase in net arrivals since the *coup d'état* of 1932, amounting to 8,000 in 1935-36, 11,000 in 1936-37, and 23,000 in 1937-38. According to official population estimates for 1937, the number of Chinese in Thailand at that time was 524,062.[12] But according to an independent estimate, the number of Chinese residents may have been over a million and a half. The seeming contradiction between reports of sharpened antagonism to Chinese residents and increasing numbers of arrivals in the 'thirties is explained with the fact that the economic discrimination operated almost entirely to the disadvantage of merchants but not that of general laborers, servants, and professional workers. The proportion of persons engaged in commerce was 87 per cent among the Chinese immigrants in 1937, 68 per cent in 1938, and only 49 per cent in 1939.

Hostility to Chinese residents in Burma was less pronounced than that to Indians, although the former had, in the decade 1920 to 1930, increased twice as fast. The reason is that the Chinese, many of them married to Burmese wives and assimilated to Burmese ways, had become essential to the country's

---

[11] The present population has been roughly estimated as probably exceeding half a million. All these computations leave out of account the large admixture of Chinese blood, especially among the Tonkinese.

[12] *Statistical Yearbook of Thailand,* No. 21, 1938-39.

commerce and industry, took little part in politics, and offered a counterpart of ties with a neighboring power to the involuntary ties with India and the British Empire. With the building of the Burma Road and the beginning of the Burma-Yunan Railroad in 1938 and 1939, and especially with the accumulating evidences of the Chinese government's intention to settle and develop the frontier region, old fears long latent revived.[13] Popular imagination exaggerated the volume of overland immigration that was actually taking place. Of some 130,000 Chinese employed in connection with the establishment of the new "lifeline," not more than 50,000 or 60,000 had actually settled down. But above all, Burmese patriots feared to have their country become involved in the Sino-Japanese War; and the growing traffic in armaments arriving in British ships gave rise to protests by the anti-British Myochit Party. Many were alarmed when Chinese agents seemed to be snapping up all available goods, accommodations, and motor vehicles, when Rangoon—as one newspaper said—had become "a second Shanghai."

Actually, the number of Chinese residents in Rangoon in 1941 was no more than 36,556, only about 6,000 more than in 1931. At that time the Chinese minority of Burma consisted of 194,000 persons,[14] two-thirds of them male, about one-third of them living close to the Chinese border in the Shan and Wa States. The importance of the group lay in the part they played in the non-agricultural sector of Burma's economy. They made up almost one-fourth of the miners, one-tenth of those engaged in trade, in banking, in metalwork, in hotel and restaurant services. They also were popular in such professions as dentistry.

In September, 1941, after the new immigration agreement with

[13] According to persons who know the Border Region, the part of Yunnan to be served by the proposed railroad is potentially richer in resources and much more likely to attract Chinese settlers than the adjoining parts of Upper Burma. (See Lawrence K. Rosinger, "Yunnan, Province of the Burma Road," *Far Eastern Survey*, XI, 2 (January 26, 1942), 19-23.

[14] The Burmese census report for 1941 states that 178,000 persons out of a total population of 16,800,000 give Chinese as their principal language. This would seem to confirm the testimony of many writers on Burma that the Chinese, whose blood is visibly evident everywhere, have merged so successfully with the native population that only immigrants or their immediate offspring constitute a recognized minority.

India had been signed (see p. 61), a delegation of Burmese ministers—the first ever permitted by the British authorities to carry on direct negotiations with a foreign power—arrived in Chungking and were reassured by the Chinese government of its desire to keep emigration to Burma within modest bounds and to take no unilateral action in the often-discussed improvement of the boundary between Yunnan and the Northern Shan States. These assurances have often been repeated since, though for the present they are of no immediate practical importance.

In Netherlands India, one of the few countries of the region to have a reliable decennial census, the Chinese population grew by 2.44 per cent between 1905 and 1920, and by 4.31 per cent between that year and 1930, when the total stood at 1,233,000. There was a considerable decrease in the number of arrivals of Chinese immigrants between the five-year periods 1925-29 and 1930-34, with further decreases in 1934 and 1936, and slight rises in the next two years. In Netherlands India, the role played by the Chinese is more like that in the Philippines than like that in British Malaya. Almost one-half of them live in towns and cities. On the plantations of Sumatra they are gradually being replaced with Javanese labor.[15] Throughout the Outer Provinces, especially in Borneo, Sumatra, Celebes, and the Moluccas, Chinese farm colonies can be seen. These are sometimes made up of former plantation laborers on the first step toward independence. It is to be feared, however, that the land is owned by Chinese absentee landlords who, as is their habit, take the cream.

Our account of the war's effect on the fortunes of the Chinese overseas communities and on the movement of migration between them and southern China must of necessity be brief. Between 1937 and 1941, the revival of trade in Southeast Asia had a favorable effect, as we have seen, on the demand for Chinese labor. But emigration from South China seems to have fluctuated also with the fortunes of war. During this whole period, the Chinese communities in the Nan Yang, no less than

[15] At the end of 1938, only 4.4 per cent of the coolies on the East Coast of Sumatra, the oldest plantation area, were Chinese; and even of these a large proportion were employed, not on plantations, but by lumber camps owned by Singapore Chinese. J. H. Boeke, *The Structure of Netherlands Indian Economy*, New York, 1942, pp. 152-3.

the relatively much wealthier ones on other continents, were a tower of strength to the national government.[16] And, being near, they were able to do even more than make gifts and purchase war bonds. Many of them went back to serve in the Army or in the civil service, wherever they could be of use. Almost all of those who stayed behind boycotted Japanese goods and used their influence with native and European neighbors to do likewise. Some staged strikes against the export of minerals and other potential war materials to Japan.

During and after the Japanese conquest of Southeast Asia, the Chinese population stood loyally by its allies, and with them suffered the loss of home and business and means of livelihood. With the Japanese seizure of Indo-China began that systematic destruction of Chinese enterprise and property abroad which is part of the war's history and which has greatly impoverished civilization all around the South China Sea. To what extent Chinese citizens were able to return to China before they were cut off, or when to do so meant to break through the Japanese lines, we do not know. Between January and May, 1942, 1.3 million Chinese returned to the homeland through the four provinces of Fukien, Kwangtung, Yunnan, and Kwangsi. The Overseas Affairs Commission during that time spent Ch. $34,000,000 on emergency relief, and the Executive Yuan expected this fund eventually to reach $100,000,000. Some of this was spent through international organizations to help in the repatriation of emigrants, to provide for the continued training of students, to relieve families normally dependent on remittances from overseas.[17]

[16] It is mainly to the old-established Chinese communities that the credit belongs for contributions from overseas to the Chinese war effort, amounting to Ch. $213,500,000 for the two and a half years, July, 1937, to December, 1939. According to Pai Tsu-yee, assistant manager of the Bank of China, Chinese residents in the Nan Yang countries between 1937 and 1941 subscribed to one-fifth of the five hundred million dollar National Salvation Bonds.

[17] Reports on relief disbursements to refugees from overseas by the National Relief Commission and the Overseas Affairs Commission do not refer exclusively to those returned from the *Nan Yang* (Southeast Asia) but also those arrived from Shanghai and Hong Kong. Up to the end of June, 1942, 1,193,170 persons had benefited from this fund. The great majority of them

There has been a continuing trickle of returning emigrants by sea, but their number cannot have been large. Even fewer were those Chinese residents of enemy-occupied countries in Southeast Asia who were able to reach British possessions or Dominions. For example, only 1,300 Chinese from the British and Netherlands colonies in the western Pacific are known to have reached India, and six hundred of these have subsequently reached China. Only a few hundred found shelter in Ceylon, in Australia, and in New Zealand. In May, 1942, several thousand Chinese returned from the Nan Yang formed in Chungking an association for the twofold purpose of giving war-time relief to those of their number who were in need, and of planning for the reconstruction of Chinese enterprise overseas. Needless to say, this organization has the blessing of the Chinese government, which, indeed, has done everything possible to encourage it.

Another hardship suffered by Chinese residents in the countries of Southeast Asia has received all too little attention. Many thousands of them were the main supports of large families in China, especially in the densely populated coastal communities of Kwangtung and Fukien. With the Japanese occupation they lost the opportunity of continuing the regular and well-organized remittances home to which they were accustomed.[18] According to Japanese broadcasts, the ban on home remittances to China from Malaya and Indo-China was lifted in 1944 presumably to

were in Kwangtung and Kwangsi, less than 4,000 in Yunnan. "As many of the refugees as possible were repatriated to their ancestral villages and towns." (Ministry of Information. *China after Five Years of War*, New York, 1942, pp. 172, 174.) As the relief was intended mainly for technical workers, teachers, and students, it is not surprising that almost as much of the appropriations was allocated to Yunnan as to Kwangtung Province.

[18] The use of these remittances is described by Ta Chen in *Emigrant Communities in South China*, New York, 1940, pp. 73-85. Although many attempts have been made to estimate the total amount of these payments, not even an approximate figure can be hazarded; for, the recorded transactions include payments for goods received, investments, and patriotic gifts as well as contributions to the living expenses of their families. The most recent estimate of the total remittances is one given out on May 10, 1942, by Liu Wei-chih, Minister of Foreign Affairs. He stated that for twenty or thirty years prior to the outbreak of the Sino-Japanese War the annual cash remittances to China from overseas Chinese had averaged Ch. $300,000,000 —an amount far exceeding the country's unfavorable trade balance.

lessen the distress occasioned by their lack in the Japanese-occupied provinces.

As to other prospects of postwar migration between southern China and the countries of Southeast Asia, opinions are divided. Some expect a severe depression in precisely those industries, rubber and tin, in which Chinese capital and labor have been prominent, as substitute sources and materials will have come into use.[19] Another pessimistic forecast is that nationalist and anti-foreign movements are likely to grow in adversity. And third, colonial as well as national authorities will consider the occasion of a general reshuffle of international relations opportune to add to the economic and social protection of their subjects by making their immigration laws and regulations stricter than before. In order to create a more balanced economy the legislators and administrators will also try, through appropriate measures and credit institutions, to reduce and if possible eliminate the parasitic activities of some of the "alien oriental" groups.

On the other hand, just because of the disturbed condition, a population with considerable experience of mobility, like that of South China, would be able to take advantage of new opportunities. We have already remarked in passing that if the British-Indian conflict should not be adjusted to the satisfaction of both sides, British employers in Malaya and Burma, in planning new enterprises or reopening old ones, may wish to substitute Chinese for Indian labor. Similarly, they might be expected—since such people do not often take a very long view—to prefer Chinese to Javanese labor if there were any danger of a strong nationalist independence movement growing up among the latter. In this connection it should be remembered that the major flow of Chinese labor emigration in recent years has not been to Thailand, the Philippines, or Netherlands India, where a bitter anti-Chinese feeling has developed, but to British Malaya where a labor shortage, when it does arise, usually is of considerable dimensions and permits of no delay.

The politics of united action on the part of the United Nations in postwar reconstruction will become a factor of importance. As hinted before, a demand for labor in British Malaya and an

[19] Philip E. Lilienthal and John H. Oakie, *Asia's Captive Colonies.* Pamphlet, New York, 1942, pp. 44-5.

oversupply of labor in Java admirably supplement each other. Even an informal economic and administrative collaboration between the two dependencies would suffice to lay the basis for a comprehensive Javanese settlement in Malaya. The relations between the European powers and China also will require careful consideration. It seems hardly likely that Great Britain could afford the luxury, immediately the war is over, of hitting China in a very sensitive spot by adding Malaya to the zone barred to the Chinese labor immigrant—whether directly or indirectly by cutting off the chances of employment.

As for the world market's capacity after the war to absorb in large quantities the typical products of tropical Asia, it may not be overoptimistic to anticipate that a limited flow of capital would be more likely to go into fully equipped established plants, ready for production, rather than the creation of new ones. Unless cheaper substitutes should already have become strongly established, the Asiatic rubber plantations will not suffer from a lack of markets—and this especially not if we take into account the changing character of transportation—for example, the vast number of tire-equipped vehicles constructed for war uses that can be reconditioned for many varieties of civil use. For some years, on the same ground that it will be most economical to use existing facilities and equipment instead of immediately starting costly new projects, and especially until agriculture in the war-devastated areas can be brought back to its former productivity, tropical food products are likely to be in at least as great demand as they were before the outbreak of the war. And it can hardly be doubted that during the emergency of several years enough tonnage will be made available to permit of large shipments.

In other words, while the prospect is by no means clear, some of the outlets for Chinese emigration in Southeast Asia may have to be written off for the future. Other outlets may be expected to be transformed from opportunities for permanent settlement into opportunities for seasonal labor migration and for other short-term labor contracts. The compensating advantages of the gradual disappearance of labor exportation as the traditional relief of overpopulation in South China include, above all, the flow back into China's home provinces of capital, talents, and energies which have benefited the mother country too little in the past. If the national government will be strong enough to keep the divisive elements in the southern provinces under control, to oust corruption and *laisser faire* from provincial and local government, to introduce a more equitable system of taxation and those fundamental agrarian reforms without which there can be no security—a very large if—the people of the densely populated coastal belt should be able, without aid from above, to absorb the present surplus population in remunerative enterprise of many sorts.

It is, of course, theoretically possible to deflect the flow of migration from overseas into the interior. However, seeming precedents for such a movement in Chinese history do not apply. The rice-growing lowland people, however hard pressed, have never in large numbers gone into the mountainous western country. The people of the southern coastal region, because of their longer and more intimate contacts with the outside world, are farther advanced than those of the hinterland in what might be called pre-industrial intensification of agriculture and of crafts. Fukien, with its mineral resources and water power, would have become a budding Chinese New England, had not in the course of the last thirty years promising enterprises engineered by its returned emigrants time and again suffered shipwreck on the rocks of official corruption, social disorder, and plain greed. South China needs social peace and honest government, not avenues of escape.

8

EMIGRATION FROM NORTHERN CHINA AND KOREA

Northern China

IN THE NORTHWESTERN PROVINCES of China overpopulation is largely explained with the oppression and impoverishment of the people in the latter days of the Manchu regime though the interference of foreign powers with their special concessions, extraterritoriality, and pressure of armed forces made matters worse. The neglect of river conservancy and irrigation, excessive multiple taxation, and other consequences of weak and corrupt government laid waste once-flourishing arable districts, reduced production, created tenancy and a landless proletariat, and eventually led to ruinous sequences of floods and famines, banditry and civil strife. As a result of these various causes—which some historians may prefer to describe as themselves the effects of an excessive rate of reproduction—the rural population density in some parts of Shantung is now around three thousand per square mile.

Manchuria was kept a sparsely populated reservoir for the imperial race and closed to Chinese immigration. Yet, in 1900 it was estimated that four-fifths of the Manchurian population was Chinese.[1] This means that there must have been considerable seepage across the border long before immigration was legally permitted (see above, p. 3). After the fall of the dynasty, the northern war lords augmented the natural flow of Chinese colonists by recruiting among the impoverished peasants below the Wall laborers for mining and transportation. During the 'twenties, the annual arrivals of these migrants usually exceeded departures by one-fourth and in some years by two-thirds.[2] Any-

[1] Manchukuan census statistics do not list Chinese nationals as such at all.

[2] Franklin L. Ho, *Population Movement to the North Eastern Frontier in China.* Pamphlet, Shanghai and New York, 1931.

one who has seen something of the social and political conditions that prevailed in the countryside of North China before the "China Incident," will probably agree that only a revolutionary change in the social order, especially in landlord-tenant relations and in local taxation, could arrest a migration movement which has become for the masses the only form of relief. Even if by some unforeseen stroke of fortune a reform government were to come in tomorrow, emigration from that area would still have to continue; for, without at least a partial relief of population pressure those constructive measures that are necessary to make life tolerable for the ordinary peasant would be very difficult to apply.

Manchuria is the logical haven to receive these refugees. It is as yet far from being populated to capacity. Even without any five-year plan and without large foreign capital investments, it can support a much larger farm population. The great majority of Chinese immigrants have stayed close to existing population centers instead of settling in those undeveloped districts where virgin land still awaits the pioneer's spade. They have always been herded to work for low wages or as tenants on inequitable terms to enrich those landowners who had the police force of the provinical governments at their beck and call.[3]

The Japanese occupation of Manchuria in 1932 and the ruthless suppression of freedom under the puppet regime which followed broke down the formal channels of migration from China.[4]

Obviously as a military and police measure, the doors were closed for a time to all labor migration. The influx of Chinese laborers and members of their families suddenly fell from a quarter of a million in 1930 to a net admission of only six thousand in 1931 and a net egress of 85,000 in 1932. In the next two years, the Japanese administration actively recruited laborers in China for railway building and other public works, with the

[3] Chen Han-seng, *Notes on Migration of Nan Min to the Northeast.* Pamphlet, Shanghai and New York, 1931.

[4] "The Chinese Peasantry under the Puppet Regime of Manchukuo," *Agrarian China,* Selected Source Materials, Chicago, 1938, pp. 216-23. There are now in China below the Wall tens, perhaps hundreds, of thousands of refugees who, though Chinese in every respect, regard Manchuria as their homeland and desire to return there as soon as the Japanese have been driven out.

result of net admissions of 135,000 in 1933 and 251,000 in 1934. In 1935, the Manchukuan government, having great difficulty with insurrection and "banditry," restricted Chinese immigration so that again there was an excess of departures in 1936 and a net admission of only 65,000 in 1937. Only since 1938, after northeastern China had been subjected, did active recruiting begin again. The Manchukuan government itself in 1937 explained its inauguration of a five-year plan—necessitating the admission of 291,000 Chinese laborers and farm workers in 1938 and 722,000 in 1939—with the fact that the Japanese war effort in China was much more difficult than had been anticipated.[5]

According to other reports, the labor requirements of Manchuria in recent war years have been far from realized. A labor association set up under the puppet administration in North China with the aim of recruiting two million laborers in that area—one and a half million for Manchuria, 150,000 for Inner Mongolia, 100,000 for Japan, and 250,000 for Japanese-owned enterprises in North China itself—fell far short of its aim. In spite of a form of recruitment verging on compulsion, Manchuria received only a million workers instead of a million and a half, and to judge from the experience of the previous four years, probably only two-thirds of the migrant workers could be induced to stay. Farmers in the areas most exposed to the operations of the recruiting agents organized themselves for self-protection and, in some instances, migrated to "safer" localities where they could engage in farming or small industries.[6] Nevertheless, the fact that over a million Chinese with 330,000 dependents could be "persuaded" in 1942 to go to Manchuria shows

[5] There was also an attempt, early in 1942, when many machine shops in Shanghai had been closed, to recruit in the International Settlement of that city mechanics and fitters for the rolling mills, airplane factories, motor assembly plants, mines, and transportation services in Manchuria. The recruiting agents met, however, with little success. An attempt made thereafter by Japanese military to requisition the services of skilled workers in the International Settlement for forced labor in Manchuria was checked by the Japanese chairman of the Municipal Council, who evidently anticipated considerable social disturbance if any such attempt were made. As a result, the movement of workers from Shanghai to Manchuria, despite unprecedented congestion and unemployment in the city, remained within very moderate limits.

[6] Report of China Information Committee, Chungking, October, 1942.

how extremely mobile the population of North China has become.[7] In 1943, according to an unconfirmed radio report, a total of 1,038,000 migrants from North China entered Manchuria—708,000 of them as individuals and 330,000 in organized bodies. Nearly all of them came from Hopei. The terms of employment have been improved, at least ampler promises are made than in the past: those who take part in the increased food production will be given land of their own.

The situation is comparable with that of the late 'twenties, when annual migration to Manchuria first reached the million mark. Now, as then, the economic opportunity which Manchuria affords the hard-pressed peasants of Hopei and Shantung is in the main that of temporary work for wages. Although many will stay on, that is not their intention when they leave home. To judge from recent reports by Chinese social scientists, the conditions of employment for Chinese immigrants were even worse under the Japanese-Manchukuan regime in the 'thirties than they have been in the past; and only the existence of intolerable social conditions at home explains why this movement to Manchuria continues.[8] It is bound to continue after the war.

Whether there will also be a renewal of spontaneous Chinese migration for settlement in Inner Mongolia is more doubtful. Such migration has taken place for centuries, whenever the northern Chinese provinces were afflicted by natural or manmade disasters. But although these provinces have in modern times been visited by an unusual number of floods and droughts, these calamities as well as those caused by civil war and banditry resulted largely from disorganization of government or simply governmental neglect. It is not at all certain that under a strong national government Chinese inland migration will not again be regulated more by pull than by push—that is, by opportunity in Mongolia and Jehol rather than by starvation. Owen D. Lattimore, well-known American authority on Mongolia, takes the

[7] Quoting a Japanese source, *Hsin Hua Tih Pao,* Chungking, reported on January 19, 1943, that a total of 1,038,477 male adults had been sent to Manchuria from North China in 1942.

[8] "The Chinese Peasantry under the Puppet Regime of Manchoukuo," *Agrarian China,* ed. by R. H. Tawney, Chicago, 1940, pp. 216-23. "The Peasant Exodus from Western Shantung," *ibid.,* pp. 247-51.

view that the areas suitable for agriculture are saturated with population, anyhow, and could not receive a large addition of Chinese settlers under any circumstances. But even commercial opportunity north of the Great Wall, though it can absorb only a few thousand persons, may be economically important for North China. Historically, Chinese settlements among the Mongols have always started in that way; only a few spots in that bare and windswept region attracted agriculturists.

The English geographer P. M. Roxby, evidently under the influence of the political situation at the time he was writing, expressed the view in 1931 that the "effective occupation" of Inner Mongolia not only was "the first step towards a close settlement of the vast outlying 'province' of Sinkiang (Chinese Turkestan)," but also offered special opportunities of mixed and pastoral farming.[9] He quoted an article in the *Chinese Economic Journal* to the effect that the four Inner Mongolian provinces have a population capacity of over twenty-five million, and Sinkiang—with a population of probably less than four million— of another twenty million. Such estimates rest on too theoretical a foundation to be taken very seriously, considering the large costs that would be involved in the public works necessary to make large potential areas of arable land available to the settler through irrigation. But an era of peace and order would tend to increase the flocks of sheep and herds of other domestic animals, so gradually producing a flourishing wool trade which, in turn, might be the nucleus for a gradually expanding Chinese rural colonization. This process, Lattimore points out, would be greatly aided by improvements of the transportation facilities.[10] A revival of the Mongolian wool trade would also be one more means of raising the capacity of the North Chinese provinces themselves to support their present population with a mixed economy of industry and relatively intensive farming.[11]

There have always been small numbers of Chinese residents in Japan. At times Chinese students went to Japanese universities

[9] A memorandum prepared for the Fourth Conference of the Institute of Pacific Relations, unpublished.

[10] Owen Lattimore, *Inner Asian Frontiers of China*, New York, 1940, p. 98.

[11] See below, p. 120.

in considerable numbers; but throughout the 'thirties, the group of Chinese intellectuals in Japan diminished for political reasons; even temporary Chinese visitors were treated with little courtesy long before the outbreak of open hostilities in North China in 1937. The permanent Chinese community in Japan, treated as an inferior minority, and engaged in small trades and household work, may not exceed a few hundred.

In Soviet Asia, according to the 1939 census, the total number of Chinese is 29,620. Most of these reside in the Maritime Territory and are thoroughly assimilated, enjoying all the same rights as Russians. They retain their cultural autonomy and publish a newspaper in romanized Chinese. These Soviet citizens represent the remnant of a much larger colony of Chinese in Czarist days, many of whose members, deprived since the Revolution of remunerative trade opportunities or too individualistic to fit into a collective farm system, preferred to invoke their Chinese citizenship and return to China. Since 1920 the frontier has been closed to all further immigration.

Korea

LIKE OTHER ASIATIC PENINSULAS, Korea has a long history of immigration and emigration. It was populated from the north and from China to the west. Its fertile southern lowlands attracted would-be conquerors from every direction, but for many centuries it managed to carry on a precarious independent existence. In its turn it helped to civilize Japan, to which it gave many of those arts which are now cherished by that country's panegyrists as characteristic fruits of the native genius. It also sent forth an occasional population surplus to people some of the fertile valleys beyond its northern mountain frontier and to extend its fishing into northern waters. The growth of population did not keep within the bounds set by the country's natural resources and the state of the people's arts. Famine and pestilence took their toll.[12]

[12] William Elliot Griffis, one of the more reliable of foreign observers before the Japanese domination, intimates that there was in Korea also a form of voluntary limitation of births; the rules of costly mourning and of postponement of marriage for several years on the death of parents and

Since 1910, the internal and external migrations of Korea have been dominated by brutal conquest. In the first decade of Japanese occupation, hundreds of thousands of Korean farmers were squeezed from the best arable land to less and less desirable land and, many of them, off the land altogether.[13] Those who did not become tenant farmers for Japanese landlords were forced to submit as wage-earners to the humiliating labor conditions imposed on them by Japanese employers. And more than a million of them became the pawns of Japan's expansionist policy in Manchuria and North China. This controlled movement of migration was used not only for economic purposes, but also to clear out of Korea as much as possible of the element active in opposition to Japanese rule.

Manchuria benefited from the distress of native farming in Korea under Japanese sovereignty since 1910 by a steady influx of agricultural immigrants who have done much to improve the land in the provinces of Chien Tao and Kirin. Jurisdiction over these immigrants, first only in the South Manchuria Railway Zone but later in all parts of Manchuria, was one of the hottest objects of dispute between Japan and China ever since 1910. In 1909, the Tumen River had been recognized as the boundary between China and Korea, and an area in the Chien Tao district had been opened up for Korean colonization, with the proviso that the Korean immigrants were to submit to the laws of China. With the annexation of Korea, however, Japan claimed that these emigrants were subjects of the Mikado and entitled to the "protection" of extraterritoriality and consular jurisdiction. By the Sino-Japanese Treaty of 1915, most of the rights which the Japanese claimed were conceded; they included the permission of unlimited immigration and leasing of land on the part of Koreans. After that, the Korean emigrant farmers more and more became Japan's cat's-paws in continued pressure on China

grandparents, and other hindrances imposed by tradition to early marriage or its consummation. Of these he gives graphic examples. (*Corea, the Hermit Nation,* New York, 1888, pp. 280-3.)

[13] The story is told by Hoon K. Lee in *Land Utilization and Rural Economy in Korea,* Chicago, 1936. See also Andrew J. Grajdanzev, *Modern Korea,* New York, 1944, for the use of deportation to put malcontents under control; "Korea's Population," *The Voice of Korea,* I, 9 and 10 (April 14 and 27, 1944).

for more rights. Apart from the natural fear of the Chinese nationals of aggressive designs on the part of Japan, which gave Japan some cases of actual violation of treaty stipulations on their part, there were concrete disputes around such matters as water rights, all of them played up by the Japanese "protectors" of the Korean immigrants far beyond their intrinsic importance.[14]

The Korean colony in Manchuria grew from about 53,000 in 1910 to 459,000 in 1920, 607,000 in 1930, 662,000 in 1935. Inclusive of the former South Manchuria Railway Zone, the Korean population of Manchuria was 775,000 in 1935 and 1,162,000 in 1939.[15] With the growing labor shortage in Japan since 1937, Korean migration to Manchuria has been limited to a maximum of 10,000 a year.

The conditions of the Korean settlements in Manchuria under the present regime seem to have steadily deteriorated. The same "concentration village" method which was introduced to keep down "banditry" among Chinese residents (both immigrant and Manchurian nationals) was also introduced in 1933 to regiment the Korean farmers. But apparently the great majority of them remained free to carry on in their scattered villages. Another attempt to gain greater control over the Korean population took the form of farm settlements strung out along certain railway lines. But again the experiment seems to have remained of small dimensions, despite a nominal capital investment of thirty million yen. The scheme is similar to that of various land-development companies for Japanese emigrants abroad: provision is made for loans, equipment, houses, schools, clinics, and policing. On the four settlements for Koreans started by the East Asia Development Company before the undeclared war in China interrupted the flow of Japanese capital into this venture, a total of 2,500 families had been settled in 1936. No plans were under way for

[14] C. Walter Young, *Korean Problems in Manchuria as Factors in the Sino-Japanese Dispute*, Supplementary Document No. 9 to Report of the Commission of Enquiry (Lytton Commission), 32 pp., Geneva, 1935.

[15] Japanese estimates of Korean population, both in the homeland and in other parts of the Japanese empire, are uncertain and sometimes contradictory. The figure given in the text for Koreans in Manchuria is probably approximately correct, and it may be assumed that the number of expatriates has grown since then. See Nym Wales, "Rebel Korea," *Pacific Affairs*, XV, 1 (March, 1942), 25.

additional settlements, though the project originally called for the settlement of a million Koreans; but even in 1936 it was planned to draw a majority of the colonists from among Korean farmers already settled in Manchuria. The Governor General of Korea, as head of the colonization society, used some of its funds to draw labor from southern to northern Korea.

In the Soviet Union there are, according to the census of 1939, 180,412 Koreans. Most of them until 1937 lived in the Maritime Territory, close to Vladivostok. In that year almost the whole colony was transplanted to Siberia and Central Asia.

Migration into Russian-owned territory started as early as 1867 when flood and famine devastated some of the kingdom's densely populated farm areas. Unlike Chinese immigration, which was largely that of single men without families, the Koreans came in family and village groups. Czarist policy toward Korean immigration vacillated between an eager welcome for cheap labor and fear of "yellow" penetration. Even before the Japanese annexation of Korea, strong measures were taken to exclude Koreans and, wherever possible, to replace them with Chinese. As a result, the Korean society of the Maritime Province split socially into two factions: those thoroughly assimilated who had become Russian citizens, usually owned land, and even filled civil service positions, and those who were barely tolerated and exploited as small farmers and landless laborers. The latter subsequently were courted by Japanese propagandists as Asiatics who on occasion had suffered from Russian oppression and were ripe material for a pan-Asiatic movement.[16]

This explains not only the closing of the frontiers to further Korean immigration after the establishment of the Republic, but also the removal of most of the Korean families, together with those of other nationalities and even Russian ones, from the Maritime Territory to Central Asia. One such resettled Korean group has successfully initiated a rice-growing collective enterprise in Uzbekistan. The great majority of the Korean residents, however, had become thoroughly assimilated in maritime Siberia. They conducted their own collective farms, carried on schools, even higher schools, in the Korean language, and served in the

[16] Jean Morton, "The Koreans of the Soviet Far East," *China Today*, III, 9 (June, 1937), 126-9.

Army—some of them as officers. Many of them will wish to return to the milder climate of their former home when this has been freed of foreign rule.

The stream of Korean emigrants was diverted to Japan itself under the necessity, first, of preparation for war and, then, of war itself. What had been a thin trickle of Korean immigration became a mighty stream. From 3,000 in 1913 and 41,000 in 1925, the number of Korean residents in Japan rose to 419,000 in 1930, 800,000 in 1939, and about a million in 1942. For the great majority of landless laborers, migration to Japan in the earlier years of this movement was an improvement of their condition, since the oversupply of idle labor in Korea itself made for wages considerably below those paid in Japan. It appears from the reports of Korean refugees that, except to the extent to which they share the general distress of Japan at war, the material lot of the Korean immigrants has improved a little, although they are still admitted only to the lowest-paid jobs: they are now essential workers, not only in food production, but also in war industries.

Korean labor crews have been mentioned as surrendering to Allied occupying troops in New Guinea and on various island groups taken by the Japanese in the southward and eastward advance. Even larger numbers will be found to have been engaged, under compulsion, in the construction of air fields and other Japanese military works as the campaign shifts to Formosa and other outposts in the China Sea. Some of these labor troops may have been transferred from China rather than from Korea itself, which is short of labor power. Both Chinese and Korean labor gangs have been sent to Hokkaido, but the Korean ones probably more numerous. The labor camps are conducted, apparently, on the Nazi model, and the wages paid in Japanese currency will have little value when remitted or taken home to Korea. Labor "recruits," according to the testimony of Americans returned on the *Gripsholm*, are bound to accept any assignment, anywhere.

In Occupied China (not including Manchuria), about 100,000 Koreans, mostly males, made up the bulk of the non-Japanese labor force under Japanese control at the time of maximum activity. Though some may have been attracted by what seemed promising opportunities of employment, most of these laborers were sent practically under duress. Almost none of them are able to make more than a bare living. It is known that some of them will wish to remain in China at the end of the war unless economic conditions in Korea should at once greatly improve. They could be absorbed at home only in industry and trade, as for some time to come agriculture will suffer from an excess of man power.

9

EMIGRATION FROM JAPAN

IN THE CASE OF JAPAN even more than in that of China, the profusion of available literature makes it unnecessary to discuss at length the causes and the nature of its population movements.[1] As in China, emigration was illegal until modern times. It did not really begin until after Japan had become an imperialistic power and desired to settle Japanese citizens in conquered territories. This began with the acquisition of the Kurile Islands from Russia in 1875, the seizure of the Lu Chu Islands in 1876, and—on a larger scale—the wresting from China of Formosa and the Pescadores in 1895.

[1] Among the more important recent works are E. F. Penrose, *Population Theories and Their Application*, Stanford University, 1034; Ryoichi Ishii, *Population Pressure and Economic Life in Japan*, Chicago, 1937; Shiroshi Nasu, *Aspects of Japanese Agriculture*, New York, 1941 (*passim*); Marcel Requien, *Le Problème de la Population au Japon* (Bull. de l'Ecole Franç. d'Extrême-Orient), Paris, 1934; E. B. Schumpeter and E. F. Penrose, chapters in *The Industrialization of Japan and Manchukuo, 1930-1940*, New York, 1940; Karl J. Pelzer, *Economic Survey of the Pacific Area*, Part I; *Population and Land Utilization*, New York, 1941; Jesse F. Steiner, "Population Trends in Japan," *American Sociological Review*, IX, 1 (February, 1944), 36-40; Allan B. Cole, "Japanese Population Problems in War and Peace," *Pacific Affairs*, XVI, 4 (December, 1943), 397-417.

The history of Japanese emigration to Formosa is interesting because on a smaller scale it illustrates the major characteristics of the later and larger attempts to colonize Korea and Manchuria. In 1905, Japanese nationals formed 2 per cent of the population, and in 1938 5.8 per cent.[2] Chinese emigration to Formosa was prohibited in 1895, except for seasonal labor and other small classes. The disproportion between the Chinese and the Japanese population, after forty-three years of Japan's sovereignty, has two causes: the natural increase of the Chinese between 1905 and 1937 was one of 25 per cent, that of the Japanese one of 19 per cent; Japanese farmers and fishermen, notwithstanding many inducements offered them by their government, refused to go to Formosa or, if they did go, to stay there. In some of the early years of the occupation the number of Japanese departures almost equaled that of the subsidized arrivals. The first batch of Japanese immigrants seem to have been typical adventurers and grabbers of land grants. Some of these people the government later was at some pains to repatriate. A better-planned land-settlement scheme in 1910 resulted in less than 3,500 actual settlements. Even the establishment of a sugar factory which started with the settlement of 78 families had attracted only 156 families by 1931. In 1936, the number of *bona fide* agriculturists, with members of their families, was only 8,000 in a total Japanese population of 282,000.

This rather astonishing end result is typical of all attempts to settle Japanese farmers in Japanese dependencies. The farm settlements remain small; the urban settlements grow. In the decade 1927 to 1936, the Japanese population of Formosa increased by 39 per cent, that of Korea—which is by far the largest—by 34 per cent, that of Kwantung and the South Manchuria Railway Zone by 100 per cent, that of the mandated islands by 460 per cent, and that of Manchuria by more than 1,000 per cent. In other words, the increase is in proportion to vocational opportunities in administration and business—with perhaps a little industry, too, to account for the growth in Manchuria. But the great majority of these colonists are not, or do not remain, manual workers.

[2] The above and following data are taken from *Formosa Today*, by Andrew J. Grajdanzev, New York, 1942.

Not counting combat forces, the estimated number of Japanese in the major dependencies and occupied territories, in October, 1942, was as follows:

Korea		700,000
Manchuria		700,000
Formosa		310,000
Occupied China		600,000
North China	410,000 [3]	
Central China	160,000	
South China	30,000	
Southern Territories		58,000
Indo-China	2,000	
Thailand	2,500	
Burma	1,000	
Malaya	7,500	
Netherlands Indies	15,000	
Philippines	30,000	
Total		2,368,000 [4]

In Korea, the Japanese make up less than 3 per cent of the population. Seven out of every ten live in one of the fifty cities of the country, and one out of every two in one of the large cities.

Without a full knowledge of the purpose that has guided the

[3] A Japanese estimate for August, 1943, mentions 376,000 Japanese nationals in North China. The newspaper *Ta Kung Pao* gives the number of Japanese in China as 640,000 at the end of September, 1943, two-thirds of them in North China, most of the rest in Central China.

[4] This enumeration does not include the 313,000 Japanese named in 1936 as residing in Sakhalin (Karafuto). Presumably this territory, with some of the island groups, is included in Japan Proper; yet it is entirely colonial in character. Two out of every three of the Japanese residents live in cities with more than ten thousand population. The interior of the peninsula remains practically uninhabited, there being only a few hundred natives. Apart from some 15,000 persons engaged in administration and transport, the rest are employed in coal mining, canning, paper-making, and small industries. A German visitor reports that most of the Japanese immigrants seem to have gone there to escape debts and mortgages, but that "every settler yearns for home." Nevertheless, there are almost as many females as males, and the birth-rate is high. (Martin Schwind, "Hauptfragen um Japanisch-Sakhalin," *Zeitschrift für Erdkunde*, VIII, 11-12 (1940), 286-91.

various attempts of the Japanese government to settle Japanese peasants in Manchuria, it is difficult to speak of the results in terms of success or failure. It is true, the numbers actually placed have not been large; and the disappointment of the government in this respect appears from the fact that various plans have followed each other to speed up the program. As recently as 1936 the Overseas Ministry adopted a plan for sending a total of one million Japanese families (five million persons) to Manchuria, under the auspices of the Manchuria Colonization Joint Stock Company, but by August, 1943, only about 57,000 households of Japanese farmers had actually been distributed among the 573 training projects set up to receive and prepare them for their pioneer life, in addition to some 65,000 youth volunteer workers and 38,000 members of the national labor service who may or may not have been seriously intended for land settlement.

The colonization scheme was worked out in great detail. It distinguished between group settlements consisting of from two to three hundred households and collective settlements formed by from ten to fifty households. The subsidies offered for travel and equipment under the first five-year plan were too small, and a second five-year plan, adopted in 1943, increased them besides providing for better medical care, better selection of sites, better training of leaders. But by then the need for greater food production in Manchuria had become so great that all "pampering" of the recruited settlers ceased. Scientific managers were brought in to direct the agricultural labors of Manchurian and Chinese conscripts and of Japanese "volunteers" alike. Additional agricultural workers were sent from Japan, without any promise of land and government assistance, to take part in the effort to raise the Manchurian rice production by 70 per cent.

As originally conceived, settlement operations were to have been spun out over a period of twenty years, beginning with the settlement of no more than six thousand families in 1937 and 1938. In other words, there was not from the start enough capital in sight to finance a really large-scale settlement of Japanese farmers in Manchuria with the thoroughness of attention to detail and completeness of control which so appeals to the Tokyo bureaucracy. By May, 1941, a total of 22,619 families had been settled by the Japanese Department of Overseas Affairs as "self-guarding immigrants," about one-fourth of the number planned for.[5] In the Kwantung Leased Territory and the South Manchuria Railway Zone, where the Japanese had full control for many years prior to the occupation of Manchuria, and where if anywhere it might have been expedient to settle Japanese farmers, only about 1,500 families were settled by 1931. Since 1932, the Japanese population in Manchuria has nevertheless more than doubled, from 319,000 to 750,000 in 1943.[6]

Japanese emigration to foreign countries was in the prewar decade cut off by restrictions and exclusions in one country after another. In a recent peak year for emigration, 1933, 27,000 Japanese left their country, but 14,000 returned. In some years the number of returned nationals exceeded that of emigrants. The net loss of population to Japan through emigration was at no time more than a small fraction of the natural population increase.

Three circumstances impeded the growth of Japanese foreign settlements: the climate was unsuitable for the Japanese traditional styles of farming, or the territory was already densely populated, or the standards of living and hence the income requirements of competing groups were much lower than those of the Japanese settlers. There is reason to believe that the Japanese insistence on rigid government control over the emigrants, with its corollary of closed settlements, everywhere militated against their success. It aggravated if it did not create antagonism in the receiving countries.[7] Nor can normal processes of economic and social adjustment of immigrant farmers take place where their every move is dictated from political con-

[5] *Manshu Keijai*, September, 1941. Other authoritative estimates are similar. Only the *Japan Times and Advertizer*, of Tokyo, makes the unsupported claim, November 11, 1941, that 83,873 farm families had already been settled by the end of the 1941 season, as compared with 100,000 families called for by the plan.

[6] The figures are for Manchukuo, including the former Kwangtung Leased Territory and the South Manchuria Railway Zone. Since they include the military garrison, they are not very significant.

[7] For striking case illustrations see John F. Normano and Antonelli Gerbi, *The Japanese in South America*, New York, 1943.

siderations by a government a long way from the actual problems that have to be met.[8]

Almost one out of every two Japanese residents abroad (not including Manchuria) in 1937 (617,795) lived under the American flag (Continental U.S.A., 114,642; Hawaii, 151,850; Philippine Islands and Guam, 24,048). These figures include persons of Japanese race who are American nationals. Japan has never abandoned in principle (nor has China) its sovereignty over the foreign-born descendents of its nationals; and this *jus sanguinis*—with the Japanese *penchant* for disregarding agreements—may at any time be dragged out if she wishes to claim authority over Japanese residents in conquered countries.[9]

The reasons that led to the virtual exclusion of Japanese settlers from countries under occidental control vary in detail, but the underlying motive was the same:

The struggle of the laborer to protect himself against the labor competition of an alien race, which he is unable to meet successfully, is to be classified with the struggle of the Boers to protect themselves against the political encroachment and predominance of the more alert outlanders, and with an effort which is now going on in Haiti on the part of the citizens of the Black Republic to protect themselves against the business competition of foreign traders whom they are at this moment trying to exclude. The whole subject of peaceful invasion by which the people of a country may have their country taken away from them, and the analogy and contrast between the swarming of peaceful immigration and business enterprise and the popular invasions by force of arms in former times, such, for instance, as those overrunning the Roman Empire, are most interesting.[10]

Political reasons in recent prewar years outweighed purely economic ones in the raising of bars against Japanese immigrants.

[8] John E. Orchard once suggested that Japanese schemes of directed settlement in foreign countries never were intended to grow but were merely sops to popular demand. *Geographical Review,* XVIII, 3 (July, 1928), 400.

[9] The United States government has never acknowledged this right of nationality by blood and so cannot use its theoretical retention by Japan as an excuse for the discriminatory nature of its treatment of American citizens of Japanese race.

[10] Secretary of State Elihu Root, in a letter to Justice Holmes, March 6, 1907, cit. by Philip C. Jessup, *Elihu Root,* New York, 1938, II, 14.

For example, the number of Japanese residents in the Soviet Far East has decreased for some time, and there are now only about two thousand Japanese in all Siberia, including the Japanese Concessions. The Soviet government, from the start, firmly closed the door against Japanese spies and adventurers.

The growth of the Japanese colonies in the various countries of Southeast Asia was somewhat in proportion with the growth of Japanese trade. The Philippine Commonwealth was the only Asiatic country outside Japan's political control that also received agricultural colonists. But even there the actual numbers hardly justified alarm; the real danger to Philippine independence did not come from Davao. From less than five thousand a quarter of a century ago, the Japanese population of the Islands had grown to twenty-nine thousand in 1939. In Davao, 22 per cent of the area under hemp cultivation in 1936 was in Japanese control, and the great majority of immigrants actually were engaged in that industry. The colony was typical for the thoroughness of the Japanese method of making such communities self-sufficient, including carpenters, fishermen, retail merchants, hairdressers—and 47 professional photographers! [11]

Although the Japanese worked mining concessions in British Malaya, the labor force was Chinese. Nor were diverse Japanese enterprises in Netherlands India made the occasion for a large infiltration of Japanese nationals. Astonishing is Japan's feat in dominating the ocean fishing industry of the whole western Pacific without appreciably adding to the number of its residents on foreign shores. It was done by the favorite Japanese device of acquiring partnerships in native enterprises. Japanese retail trading in such countries as Netherlands India, the Philippines, and Thailand, likewise, made use of native channels. When Chinese storekeepers began to boycott Japanese goods, it would have been too late anyhow to improvise large forces of Japanese retail merchants, familiar with the local dialects and with local trading practices. A strong central organization and native affiliations alone could defeat the Chinese business man on his own ground.

In China itself the situation was different. A general estimate of the number of Japanese nationals in the three sections of

[11] A. Kolb in *Koloniale Rundschau*, November, 1938.

Occupied China has been given above (p. 99). More than one-half of the total number of 600,000 are concentrated in the large cities, two-fifths in Shanghai, Peiping, and Tientsin.[12] On October 1, 1938, the total numbers of Japanese in China was only 95,000, more than one-half of them in Shanghai and Tientsin. Since the civilian government in the occupied areas is carried on almost entirely by the Chinese puppet administrations, the great majority of the present Japanese residents are camp followers and adventurers. With a just peace settlement, restoring industrial properties in the cities to their rightful owners, but few of these *ronin* and petty tradesmen will stay behind. Their number, therefore, hardly matters, either from the standpoint of relief of population pressure in Japan or from that of population increase along the China coast. Of permanent significance is the transformation of some tens of thousands of additional Japanese nationals from the status of useful productive workers into parasites of one kind or other. One of the worst demographic by-products of the war for Japan will be the return after its defeat of substantial numbers of nationals who, during the period of expansion, have become unfitted for a useful life.

10

IMMIGRATION FROM EUROPE

AN INTERESTING TRAVEL EXPERIENCE in North China and Manchuria is to come across the cultural traces of former Russian occupation. However, the little remnant of Russian population

---

[12] "Economic Reconstruction in Occupied China," *Diamond Economic Journal*, Tokyo, July 21, 1941, p. 7 (in Japanese). Between the summer of 1941 and that of 1942, according to a more recent report, there was a further large increase in the Japanese population of some of the North Chinese cities, especially Peiping and Tientsin. The number of Japanese residents in North China as a whole was exactly ten times in July, 1942, what it had been in 1936.

after the Russo-Japanese War of 1904-05 seems to have remained more or less stationary until the World War released a wave of refugees into these areas and thence south into central China. This eastward and southward migration is roughly indicated by the following figures for the White Russian population of Harbin: 1916, 34,200; 1918, 60,000; 1922 (the peak year), 155,402; [1] 1924, 58,559. In 1932 there were still 110,000 Russians in Manchuria, 45,000 of them citizens of the Soviet Union. With the sale to Japan of the Chinese Eastern Railway in 1935 the number rapidly declined. The figure remained somewhere near 60,000 in the late 'thirties. Of the 56,000 residents in 1935, 33,000 were denationalized and 23,000 Soviet citizens.[2] There seems to have been little Russian emigration after 1922. Most of those who stayed in Manchuria are unskilled workers or persons of a formerly higher vocational status who can find only unskilled work to do. Many of them—including old employees of the Chinese Eastern Railway—lost their jobs during the political disturbance in 1932 and remained unemployed. After the sale of the Chinese Eastern Railway to Japan in 1935, most of the employees who had Soviet passports left for Russia; about two thousand of them remained in railway jobs.[3]

Because of the invasion-created unemployment and misery—a situation later repeated in North China, especially at Tientsin—the migration of White Russians continued southward to Shanghai. It was never more than a trickle, but gradually a considerable colony of White Russians formed in that city.[4] Favored as policemen and watchmen in the International Settlement, un-

[1] This figure, according to an authority resident in Harbin at that time, is exaggerated.

[2] *Contemporary Manchuria*, I, 3 (September, 1937), 19-20. According to a Manchurian census, there were still 54,000 Russians in Manchuria in 1940. George C. Gains, "Russians in Manchuria," *Russian Review*, II, 2 (Spring, 1943), 83.

[3] For a graphic description of the peculiar present situation of Russian emigrants in Manchuria, see George C. Gains, *op. cit.* An interesting account of some six thousand Cossacks who still form an independent pastoral and hunting community in the Barga frontier region is given by Bruno Plaetschke in *Osteuropa*, XI, 1 (October, 1935), 10-21.

[4] In 1930, the total number of Russians by nationality (*i.e.*, not necessarily by birth) in China Proper was 66,000, and in Manchuria 71,000, with only a few thousand spread over the other countries of eastern Asia.

willing to compete with Chinese in manual work, and few of them equipped for skilled or professional occupations, the Russian emigrés played a peculiar role in the metropolis. After the occupation of Shanghai by Japanese troops, some of the White Russians—and also Russian Jews—found their way to the Philippines, and some few eventually to the United States. But the sad remnant of a once-proud and powerful imperial group presumably still carries on as best it can in the Eastern Extension of the International Settlement and around the Avenue Joffre.

Numerically less important and of shorter duration was the influx into China of German refugees in the middle 'thirties. There were several tens of thousands of them, mostly Jews; at first mainly from Germany, then also from Poland. Some arrived by circuitous maritime routes, more by way of Siberia. About twenty thousand found their way to Shanghai and were efficiently cared for by local agencies. About one-half of the refugees settled in the French Concession and the British- and American-controlled part of the International Settlement; the other half in the Japanese-controlled part of the International Settlement. The reason for this peculiar arrangement was not love of the Japanese but the fact that both apartments and small business opportunities could more easily be found in a section of the city from which many European families had recently moved.

The only homes at first available for these Jewish refugees in Yangtzepoo and Wayside were some small houses in Chinese alleyways repaired under municipal orders and a few old foreign residences cut up into family dwellings of single rooms. More recently all European Jews have been ordered by the Japanese to move "north of the Creek"—that is, to an area of far worse overcrowding and vocational competition.[5]

Most of the German refugees regarded themselves as transients but did not have the means to move on at once. A short-

[5] For a description of the experiences of Jewish refugees in Shanghai, see Laura L. Margolis, "Race against Time in Shanghai," *Survey Graphic,* March, 1944, pp. 168-71, 190-1; also Eleanor M. Hinder, *Life and Labor in Shanghai,* New York, 1944, pp. 127-8; and Robert W. Barnett, "Shanghai's German Refugees," *Far Eastern Survey,* VIII, 21 (October 25, 1939), 251-3.

lived building boom provided jobs for some; a few with borrowed capital entered business and professional offices. When the extension of the Sino-Japanese War to Shanghai seemed imminent and many European residents of Shanghai went home, additional jobs and vocational opportunities became available to refugees. A rather grandiose scheme to settle a hundred thousand German-Jewish refugees in a closed colony in Yunnan had the general approval of the Chinese government (which had not been asked for a financial contribution) but failed to materialize. It was not a bad idea, since many of the refugees had skills that could have been utilized in the building up of industries employing local raw materials. But as the war with Japan entered its active stage, the Chinese lost interest in the European refugees; and in 1939 the governmental bodies of Shanghai, at Japanese behest, refused to admit more of these immigrants. About a thousand refugees found their way to Manila where, in 1938, a careful plan was made by a local committee to absorb them, with financial aid from New York and the rent-free lease of a farm by President Quezon. In 1939, a plan was approved by the Philippine government for the colonization of ten thousand Jewish refugees in Mindanao. Since that time, most of the German refugees in eastern Asia have remigrated and found a place of refuge in North or South America.[6] In Malaya, that is, principally in Singapore, only about two hundred Jewish refugees were left at the outbreak of the war.

The authors of a recent study of Jewish refugee migration explain the importance which Far Eastern countries assumed in the Jewish exodus from Germany, and later from Poland, with the fact that admission to them offered less difficulty than did

[6] The total number of Europeans left behind in eastern Asia after the evacuation of civilians early in the war has little bearing on the size of the European settlements, past or future; but it may be of interest that, according to a News Letter by Randall Gould, of October 7, 1942, there were at that time still between thirty and forty thousand Europeans in Shanghai, including some ten thousand German-Jewish refugees, seven or eight thousand British subjects, about fifteen hundred Americans, and most of the rest Russians. A census taken for food-rationing purposes in February of that year had shown considerably larger numbers, namely about 18,000 European refugees and nearly 30,000 Russians.

admission to many countries more easily reached.[7] For example, Shanghai was almost the only semi-European city that could be entered without a visa. Both China and Japan had in the First World War served as transit places for Jewish refugees from Germany and Lithuania who fled across Russia in the hope of reaching either an American country or Palestine. During the second exodus, however, Japan proved less hospitable.

While in the earlier war the refugees had to stay in Japan for only a few weeks until transportation was secured, the problem now grew enormously difficult because of the new visa regulations, with the result that many of the refugees had to remain in Japan for months until emigration possibilities were found. . . . With the mounting tension between Japan and the United States further complications arose, leading finally to the deportation of nearly all the refugees from Japan to Shanghai in October, 1941.[8]

Apart from the two exceptional types just described, Russian and German refugees, there has been no European labor migration toward or within eastern Asia in recent times. All but a few officials and those who have completely identified themselves with the natives may be said to be either evacuated or incarcerated or engaged in what remains of military action. This, however, is a passing situation. The number of European and American residents already had gradually diminished when war broke out between the Western powers and Japan in December, 1941. A large cause of this had been the reduction of personnel in foreign enterprises, because of the general economic depression. Only in the case of white employees on estates in Java does that situation seem to have occasioned serious distress. When white unemployed technical workers and foremen drifted to Soerabaja, it was discovered that many of them had no connections in the homeland and, in fact, were at home in Java and not in the Netherlands. Like thousands of others, they were completely identified with the life of the dependency and could not be evacuated on account of their unemployment. Most of

[7] Arieh Tartakower and Kurt R. Grossman, *Jewish Refugee*, Institute of Jewish Affairs, New York, 1944.
[8] *Ibid.*

these men will have joined the defense forces and either have been evacuated or made prisoner.[9]

While we have had a large literature concerning oriental migration to countries dominated by Occidentals, little has been written in recent times about white migration to Asia. Since the postwar era will start with almost a clean slate in this connection, it seems desirable here to summarize some of the outstanding facts and trends.

There are no good statistics for European residents in most of the countries of eastern Asia; and their numbers are relatively insignificant, anyhow. Little need be said here about the former functions of European and American residents in eastern Asia, except to indicate two important trends. The first is the increasing identification of colonials with the dependency in which they reside and which they acknowledge as their home. This is, of course, so in the case of the Eurasians, but it is also true of many thousands whose Caucasian blood is not in doubt. It is also true of those White Russians who can no longer regard themselves as exiles hoping to return to Europe. Portuguese and Spaniards, whether of pure blood or mixed (the great majority), have almost entirely merged with the dominant native groups among which they live. There are Euro-Indian-Chinese families, Jewish families with both European and oriental ancestors, French-Annamite and Dutch-Javanese groups. They are often politically and socially important but not large. There are very respectable Englishmen and Americans with Malay wives. There are military and other pensioners who know that life would not be nearly as pleasant "at home" as it is under the palms. There are reputed to be several thousand Hollanders, some of them born in Java, some in the Netherlands, who have kept their

---

[9] According to a *Netherlands News* item of September 25, 1942, all European men between the ages of 16 and 60, with the exception of those engaged in essential services, were interned in the principal cities of the Indies. Dutch, American, British, and Australian women were moved to "special residential areas." Because of their dwindling resources and their inability to obtain cash, many of them were reported to be in a precarious position. In the Philippines, according to a news item in the *Army and Navy Journal* of October 10, 1942, nearly three thousand American civilians have been interned on the campus of the Santo Tomas University where they are supplied with food by the Philippine Chapter of the Red Cross.

racial identity intact but are far too busy and happy in their profession or business to think of going away for longer than they need. As the cultures of Orient and Occident become more assimilated, and especially as the domineering type of colonial gives way to the professional whose contacts are with colleagues and students and clients of other races, as well as with laborers and menials, the type of occidental resident in the western Pacific—now no longer the misunderstood and misinterpreted "Far East"—is changing.

Connected with this trend is the second one, the larger role played by the European and American woman in eastern Asia. The general verdict seems to be that the women—especially the English- and Dutch-speaking women—have made for the estrangement of the European-American colonists from the indigenous groups with which they formerly had social contacts. But in recent prewar years this phase was passing away; and reports came more often of an *adoucement des moeurs* among the white colonials because of the presence of educated white women. This already has had appreciable social and even economic consequences, more especially in the plantation areas of British Malaya, Sumatra, and Borneo, where the influence of the white women has made for better living conditions among the contract laborers and other estate employees, for the provision of social services, and advances in social hygiene and education.

And here is the question which editors like to expound: have the triumphs of the Japanese Army and Navy in the first part of the present war undermined the prestige of the white man in eastern Asia? Indications may be deceptive. The status of the white man already was undergoing a change before this war. Reference has been made to the white resident of long standing, even of the second generation, and the more professional attitude of many of the newcomers. The white linen suit buttoned up to the chin is no longer the symbol of the superiority of the dominant race. All the artificial devices by which white residents of former generations tried to impress the multitude have tended to disappear. The eagerness of Orientals for a Western type of education proves that they no longer have mystic illusions but know where to look for the sources of some white men's superiority in some respects. And as the number of educated Orientals

110

increases, the young Occidentals, wherever born, no longer have the sense of social distance which their fathers and grandfathers had. Offenses are still being committed against native sensibilities, but nowadays they arise more often from ignorance than from arrogance. What separates the Western immigrant from the Asiatic today is, most of all, the gulf between their respective standards of living. And this will gradually fade away as, attracted by the need for technicians in modern enterprises of many kinds, the lower-income groups of Europeans and Americans come to be more fully represented in the migrant movement to Asia.

Some prophets tell us that oriental nationalism will in the postwar years decimate the number of white residents in eastern Asia. But the opposite is more likely to occur: a greatly increased influx. Measures of industrialization in several Asiatic countries and dependencies will attract in larger numbers the skilled and semi-professional groups without whose assistance the initiation of such projects would be difficult. There will still be a demand, and perhaps an increased demand, for those well paid technical advisers who live in good hotels and disappear again as soon as their task is done. But the occidental collaborator in the future is increasingly going to be a high type of manual worker. You see many such people in the Philippines and in Netherlands India. In Thailand a group of Danish workers, less than two hundred, have introduced a promising cement industry. Content with a reasonable remuneration, appreciative of the advantages of living in a low-cost country, men of this kind stay on. Some of the American mechanics in China will stay, perhaps start small enterprises of their own, draw other Americans after them.

In British Malaya, with an estimated 31,600 Europeans in 1941, it might seem that vocational opportunities for Occidentals have already been well utilized. But by far the greater part of this personnel has been employed in commerce and shipping, in the management of a few export industries, and in government. Those familiar with the situation believe that even a moderately energetic program of economic development on the peninsula would require the services of a greatly augmented group of professional workers, technicians, mechanics, and teachers. With the withdrawal of nearly all the European personnel in 1942, the opportunity for careers in Malaya will be especially great after the war. Similar opinions are expressed by persons familiar with British North Borneo and Sarawak. The North Borneo census of 1931 revealed the presence of only 340 Europeans and 236 Eurasians as against 47,800 Chinese in a native population of 205,000 nationals of Borneo and 11,500 nationals of the Malay Archipelago (probably Malays from Netherlands Borneo). Not even new agricultural industries of any importance can be developed by means of only the traditional native and Chinese skills, much less the secondary or processing industries of which some of the export crops are in need if the colony is to benefit more fully from its natural resources.

Every increase in material modernization makes life more agreeable in countries that are technically less advanced than the home country. Mass fabrication of housing units in the United States and other industrial countries will before long place on the market standardized home sections or cores, of various designs to suit life in different climates. In this way one of the greatest handicaps to comfortable living in a strange civilization may be removed. Then there is the probability of great advances in air travel after the war—not as rapid, perhaps, as some enthusiasts have pictured them, but yet substantial. This addition to his mobility will give the man of small means a far wider range of vocational opportunity than he has had in the past. It will also make life in a hot climate more bearable by permitting frequent vacations in near-by mountain resorts.

There is no reason for anticipating a sudden and sensational exchange of population between East and West. It is even possible that some doors will be closed to the white man, as he has closed doors to the Oriental. But the sort of contacts likely to be established in a period of stronger economic and political co-operation will help to overcome mutual prejudices and that sense of strangeness which in the past have kept migration for resettlement within relatively narrow limits geographically and numerically.

It is improbable that Europeans will claim the right to move in overwhelming numbers to Siberia or the Shan States or the Annamese Cordillera or some of the Sumatra highlands or even

Manchuria—although climatically all these areas compare favorably with others settled by white people. There may in theory be a certain amount of competition between potential occidental and oriental immigrants almost anywhere except in the tropical lowlands. But actually differences in standards of living, and hence in cost of labor, have closed the greater part of Asia and all of Oceania to white workers. Certain Jewish circles, it is true, in the extremity of their co-religionists' plight, have looked to western China, to Mindanao, and even to New Guinea as possible locations for large farm settlements. And so uncertain is the world outlook while the war is on that possibly one or other of these projects may yet emerge as deserving more than passing interest.[10] The Chinese, Philippine, and Netherlands Indian governments, however, have before them tasks of population redistribution of a sufficiently urgent nature to prevent their enthusiastic espousal of such plans, although all three of them have shown themselves sympathetic to the sufferings of Hitler's first and last victims.

Even for the native peoples, the possibilities of redistribution are much more limited than a mere comparison of population densities would indicate. The question is sometimes asked: if Java can stand a density of population averaging more than eight hundred to the square mile, then why cannot the much larger neighboring Outer Islands carry an at least approximately similar density, instead of an average of less than thirty? The answer lies, of course, in differences of climate and, especially, of soils. A heavy tropical rainfall, as in much of Borneo, instead of adding to the fertility of the soil, may actually denude it of its mineral content. An old formation, like that of most of New Guinea, does not produce a fertile silt as do the lavas washed from the slopes of recently active volcanoes in a large part of Java and in some parts of Celebes and Sumatra.[11]

[10] The history of New Guinea's only white colony, at Port Breton, told by Stephen W. Reed in *The Making of Modern New Guinea* (New York, 1943, pp. 292-8), is not encouraging; but some of the Jewish colonization societies have shown themselves capable of overcoming even greater difficulties than those confronted by the pioneer groups of a former generation.

[11] E. C. J. Mohr, "Climate and Soils in the Netherlands Indies," *Bulletin of the Colonial Institute of Amsterdam*, I (1937-38), 241-51. See also above, pp. 65-6.

Nevertheless, there may be areas in the tropics—probably limited in extent and only in the higher altitudes—that are actually more suited under present circumstances for white settlement than for that of natives from neighboring lowlands. This would be the case not so much on physiological grounds, though these also count, but because a high degree of technical skill and a large amount of technical equipment per capita may be required to succeed in the forms of exploitation possible there. Thus, small nuclei of white settlers may initiate enterprises—in cattle breeding or fruit growing, for example, not to speak of mixed agricultural, mining, and industrial projects—which gradually would draw in more natives or oriental immigrants and so enrich the whole economy of the region.

Again, within the compass of the present study it is possible to refer only briefly to those recent developments in tropical hygiene which have gone far to eliminate the risks of residence in hot countries for alien and native workers alike. In this connection, too, as in that of modern forms of production, the example of small nuclei of white settlement may contribute toward a rise in standards difficult to accomplish among tradition-bound native peoples. In short, instead of being exploitatory and parasitical, the role of white settlements in the tropical Far East may well be, as it has already been in the Soviet Far East,[12] that of initiation and stimulation of economic effort on the part of all population groups.[13]

[12] For example, see William Mandel, *The Soviet Far East*, New York, 1944, p. 42 *et seq.*

[13] For discussion of the still rather controversial issues surrounding the extension of white settlement to tropical regions, see A. Grenfell Price, *White Settlers in the Tropics*, New York, 1939; Isaiah Bowman, ed., *The Pioneer Fringe*, New York, 1931; and for a summary of the climate problem: Jan O. M. Broek, "Climate and Future Settlement," *U. S. Yearbook of Agriculture*, 1941, pp. 227-36.

PART IV

POSTWAR PROSPECTS

11

POSTWAR PROSPECTS IN CHINA

OUR SURVEY of China's internal migrations has shown that some of the causes which in recent times have made for an intolerable density of population in the river valleys and on the great plains may already be passing: there are possibilities of considerable alleviation of overcrowding through heightened production and a certain amount of redistribution. Whether China as a whole is overpopulated is a rather academic question when, through lack of internal transport facilities and a strong united government, the vast area called China is not yet a coherent whole. Nevertheless, with reproduction at the present rate, in so far as this can roughly be estimated, there is no prospect of an alleviation of population pressure through migration, settlement of marginal lands, or industrialization sufficient to permit a rise in living standards and to prevent a return of the Four Horsemen. The writer agrees with those population experts who predict that under a regime of economic and social reforms China will only that much faster approach the inevitable catastrophe—unless there is a considerable fall in the rate of reproduction. Yet, he is convinced that a program of reforms which would increase the expectancy of life can also be one to effect a commensurate fall in the birth-rate. There is, indeed, no other alternative to renunciation and despair than trust in those social by-products of change which are liable to escape the observation of the biologist and the statistician. Reforms which at first favor a higher rate of survival carry within them the dynamic for a rational adjustment of population to resources.

It is true, even a partial fulfillment of the Chinese government's plans for economic and social reconstruction must be expected to favor an increase in population. Two recent investigators conclude a painstaking appraisal of the outlook with these words:

The endless migratory search for new escapes from the inexorable pressure of population on resources is bound to go on for years to come. So long as uneventful periods . . . yield a rapid increase in population just so long will there be danger of recurrence of tragically eventful periods. In the past Malthusian checks have been a grim reality. Population increase has been curtailed by war, natural calamities, and disease. It will continue thus unless economic development and a curtailed natural increase work hand in hand to yield higher standards of living. In China, as in any other country, the maintenance of a desirable standard of living can only come about through a proper adjustment between resources and population.[1]

R. H. Tawney, a few years earlier, arrived at the same conclusion. Migration, he found, is not a solution of China's population problem:

Under existing conditions, the most it can do—if, indeed, it can do that—is slightly to relax the strain of abnormal local pressure, and accord a brief breathing space.[2]

The only thing sure to be effective would be a slowing down of the growth of the agricultural population. But most students of Chinese conditions are aware that the process of industrialization in China cannot be fast enough to outweigh the temporary effect of peace and agrarian reforms on the rural reproduction-rate. The immediate consequence of any improvement in social conditions, of any well-planned attack upon the sources of ill-health and inefficiency in the Chinese countryside will be a decline in the number of deaths and especially, unless other influences intervene, a greatly lessened infantile mortality. The

[1] Frank W. Notestein and Chi-ming Chiao, "Population," in John Lossing Buck, *Land Utilization in China,* Chicago, 1937, p. 397.

[2] *Op. cit.,* p. 108.

size of families will grow, and the pressure on the land soon will be as great as ever.[3] Even with great advances in public education, it is improbable that the national government, were it willing to do so, could in the near future secure a voluntary restriction in the matter of reproduction that would be commensurate with the quick response of the death-rate to even the simplest measures of public hygiene. Only greatly improved land uses and a large withdrawal of population from dependence on the land can give even temporary relief in those densely populated areas—and this means practically all the fertile soil of China—where famines and epidemics have been the only historic checks to the growth of population.

Nevertheless, it is possible that after the present war there may occur in China a combination of political and economic circumstances permitting of the introduction of measures that have proved effective elsewhere in breaking the Malthusian chain of excessive population growth and calamitous decline. There is, first of all, the possibility that China may emerge from the war with a stronger and more stable government than it has had for many decades, and that this government, freed of the necessity of preparing for defense against aggression, may be able to devote its energies solely to internal reconstruction. Large-scale projects of land reclamation and development of the transportation system, while offering no final remedy, would provide immediate relief by permitting a redistribution of population. Whether this took the form of bringing into fuller use areas now relatively sparsely populated[4] or of transferring population from marginal land to land more suitable for intensive utilization—a moot question for agrarian reformers—it

[3] A recent sample census taken in a rural county near Kunming shows that a slight degree of urbanization may have the effect of increasing the proportion of females, by drawing men off to near-by cities, with the result that the rate of reproduction is little affected. (Report of Institute of Census Research, National Tsing Hua University, Kunming, 1940, quoted in *Quarterly Journal of Library of Congress*, I, 3 (January-March, 1944), 17-21.

[4] Land reclamation and colonization projects are actually planned by the Ministry of Economic Affairs for Shensi, Szechwan, Yunnan, Kwangsi, to receive several million settlers. Other schemes are under consideration for the northwestern border region and the hilly interior of Fukien and other eastern states.

would in either case create a somewhat better immediate adjustment betwen population and resources. To be sure, no permanent gain would be achieved if the population were permitted to reproduce again quickly to the limits of the new subsistence potentiality of the land; there might be even less elasticity, and every natural adversity would fall with even greater weight upon the luckless people. But the new situation would provide a breathing space sufficient for the introduction of permanently effective interferences with the traditional cycle of births and deaths.

The special problems that must arise from the demobilization of China's enormous army must be mentioned in passing. Probably not even China's political leaders know as yet how large a standing army the country will require and be able to support after the defeat of Japan. It may be assumed that Chinese forces will take a large share in the occupation of enemy territory, so that demobilization will be spread out over a number of years. During this period possible border disturbances may have to be anticipated, and the recovery of Manchuria may provide the occasion for a re-formation of defensive forces there on a fairly large scale, with a colonization of veterans to augment these forces in case of need. The settlement of soldiers in the outposts of the empire is, indeed, a historic Chinese policy and can be resorted to again to provide nuclei for larger colonization projects. In this connection the success of the Eighth Route Army in combining self-sufficiency in food production with the reclamation of neglected lands in Shensi (see above, p. 43) may well be regarded as a proof that the old device of planting ex-soldiers, the great majority of whom are young peasants, in solid colonies can still be used to prevent the pressure of these millions on the limited resources of their native heath; at least enough of them may, with proper planning and technical assistance, thus become pioneer settlers to reduce to small dimensions the unemployment problem otherwise bound to arise from the return of so large an army to civilian life.[5]

[5] It is difficult to assess the present size of China's standing forces. The total number of men equipped with weapons of some sort is probably about three million; but the conscripted man power may run to five million or more.

Industrialization, as we know it today, usually means concentration of population. But historically industrialization has more often resulted from previous population densities that had given rise to economic and vocational specialization. Throughout China, the country town is the nucleus of a potential industrial development even though as yet its production may technically be little in advance of that in the surrounding villages. Peace, good government, and an influx of capital to make up for the former drainage of capital from most of China for safer investment elsewhere, should make possible a far greater total process of industrialization than that achieved by the development of mines and heavy industries or by the concentration of manufactures in a few huge urban aggregations. The benefits of technical advance, ever greater specialization, and so also of urban living and modernization of the way of living, can be achieved in China through a multitude of planned industrial centers, each of them taking advantage of local resources and of locally developed skills. One need not go as far as Ralph Borsodi [6] in wishing to prevent China's entry of the machine age as likely to damage her great cultural traditions, to recognize the advantage of a program of industrialization that utilizes existing concentrations of populations, insures a degree of decentralization, and prevents the further drainage of talent and capital from the ancient strongholds of Chinese civilization.

The localization of manufacturing industry in the China of today [writes R. H. Tawney in his masterly summary of China's social ills] recalls that which existed in America a century and a half ago. It clings to the eastern coast and rarely ventures into the precarious world that lies beyond the hinterland of the ports and rivers. A posture so unnatural cramps and distorts the economic and political growth of the country which suffers it. It is as though the blood which should circulate through the body were confined by a ligature within a single limb. Capital which should fertilize the resources of undeveloped areas is immobilized in a few great cities; the economic methods and social conditions of the thirteenth century continue unchanged within a few hours of the twentieth. . . . [7]

[6] "Must China Endure This, too?" *Asia and the Americas*, XLIII, 9 (September, 1943), 539-44.

[7] *Land and Labor in China*, New York, 1932, p. 137.

The new trends in industrial development the world over make for the utmost utilization of local advantages. The natural location of power sources is less important today than the availability of raw materials and the possibility to create good living conditions. Nor does the location of industrial cities depend as much as it did in the past on natural transportation facilities.

Partly also because of the lateness of China's industrialization, techniques and methods can come into play which did not exist in the Occident at the time of the Industrial Revolution. There is no need to disregard the whole large heritage of skills through an excessive mechanization of processes if the purpose is to create employment and to serve the domestic consumer market rather than to produce masses of standardized commodities for foreign markets. That the amount of capital in relation to man power available for the manufacture of commodities will be limited may prove an advantage, assuming the purpose named. A multitude of old crafts will be transformed into a multitude of small but related industries, absorbing much of the surplus labor of the region—some of it permanently, some by affording supplementary employment. New industries will be introduced—some, perhaps, to utilize in new ways local raw materials, especially fibers, that have played a small part as yet in the commodity markets of the world but are brought into use by wartime invention and experience.

In this connection, Hopei and other provinces in North China deserve special attention. Here the outlook for the development of many small industries, and the revival of some that have fallen into decay, is especially promising—always assuming a period of uninterrupted peace and order. Discussion of this outlook has been confused by too much emphasis on heavy industries. The question is often debated whether enough other mineral resources are available within this region or easily accessible to it to make possible a deflection of the coal supply of Feng Tien Sheng to help in the development of industry in China Proper. But most economists have overlooked another resource in which North China is especially rich: the variety and perfection of its skills. It has been suggested that the weaving of woolen textiles, in conjunction with a revival of sheep-raising in China itself as well as in Mongolia, would be a promising industry which already has its established nucleus both in manufacturing plants and in the homes of some villages.

There are a multitude of other crafts carried on in North China. Comparable in this respect with New England, it has because of its long winters and relative aridity long been a center of inventiveness and skill. Many of these crafts could, with small initial capital investments, be modernized and advanced to a commercial level of output and basic standardization. Such small industries, primarily engaged in the production of consumer goods for the home market, would automatically expand and absorb more labor power as the purchasing power of the Chinese farmer increased. Peiping—so often doomed by economic Cassandras—as the reservoir of many exquisite and half-forgotten arts, would resume its position as the principal fair, a sort of oriental Leipzig, for all these lesser industries and also as an art center with an assured world market.

The transition from the age-old habits and customs of the Chinese countryside and small town to those pertaining to urban industry will not be limited to a marginal population group but will at once affect large numbers. It will not be as revolutionary as that from an undisturbed rural village to a city slum, but it will carry the very elements that make for the formation of new social attitudes, especially if paralleled by a vigorous educational program.[8]

The important element in this situation, which distinguishes it from any experienced by China in the past, is that the industrial developments will take place under a unified plan, guided in all its diversity by a single policy of government and in its financial phases linked to the larger program for China's economic development. It would be easy to point out that not even the availability of transportation facilities, including motor

[8] Education, especially formal education, is not a panacea for China's ills, of course. Only quite specific measures of social conditioning will assist in the needed change of social attitudes. On the other hand, only an inadequate analysis of the known facts can produce a seeming correlation of high birth-rates with better education, such as that shown by Herbert D. Lamson (*op. cit.*, p. 554 *et seq.*). In a group of Chinese students those whose fathers are literate will tend to come from more prosperous homes than those whose fathers are not; and the larger families reported are correlated with wealth and status, not with modern education.

roads and railways, has thus far prevented the stagnation of the typical Chinese country town where traditionalism still reigns supreme.[9] And the outlook would be discouraging, indeed, if, in addition to the other favorable factors here named, there were no real prospect of a strong central government with a policy dominated by considerations of public welfare.

Again, the fact must be stressed that, together with a certain amount of redistribution of population, such industrialization pervading the Chinese hinterland as well as the coastal provinces would only ease the immediate population pressure; it would not solve the larger problem of the excessive reproduction-rate of China. The plane of living would rise, but the standard of living would not immediately change. But industrialization, and especially the industrial employment of women, would provide the setting for that psychological mobilization which alone can lift the Chinese people out of that backwardness in which historical circumstances have left them for so long. The process of social re-formation begun some thirty years ago will assume greater speed and greater thoroughness:

> The new changes . . . release the individual from the collective responsibility of the whole family and recognize in him the new rights and duties of an independent member of a larger society. The old framework has gone to pieces, not because it was incapable of holding itself together in the face of the new forces which claim its members, men or women, for the school, the factory, the shop, and the world at large.[10]

The war itself has, of course, slowed up, for the time being, the rate of reproduction. Although we have as yet little reliable information on this point, there are many indications of this.[11]

[9] For a striking case study see Ching-kun Yang, *A North China Local Market Economy*, Institute of Pacific Relations, New York, 1944, 41 pp., mim.

[10] Hu Shih, *The Chinese Renaissance*, Chicago, 1934, p. 110.

[11] The absence of men on military service makes for an unbalanced sex ratio—in the sample census quoted above, 90.7 males to 100 females (77.0 for the age group 20-30). The decrease in the birth-rate is not, therefore, as high as it would be with a temporary reduction in the number of adults of both sexes. On the other hand, the withdrawal of so many breadwinners, together with the requisitioning of food supplies and tax payment in foodstuffs, makes for an exceptionally high death-rate.

122

Dr. L. K. Tao, Director of the Institute of Social Research, is looking forward to a serious reduction of population as a result of the war, not only because of the large number of casualties in its early stages—an estimated two million killed in the first two and a half years of fighting—but more especially because of the greatly increased death-rate and the reduction of the birth-rate through large-scale evacuations and internal migration.[12]

More important in the long run will be the need which the war has shown for a much larger supply of trained industrial labor. H. D. Fong, in his study of "The Post-War Industrialization of China," says:

There has always been a great scarcity of industrial labor that will meet the urgent requirements of new industrial enterprises of all sorts. . . . Industrial labor in China as a whole did not amount to two millions even before the present war. . . . China after the war will have to launch a large-scale program of educational reform with a view to preparing the vast illiterate and agricultural population for industrial development . . . just as other newly industrialized nations, Japan for example, did many decades ago.[13]

Owen Lattimore, after a study of conditions and attitudes on the spot, declares:

It is inconceivable that Yunnan will relapse into its old lethargy. It will become one of the most profitable places in China for men of energy, ambition, and special skill or experience. For this reason it is likely to be specially attractive to Chinese from the Colonial possessions.[14]

The same theme was taken up by two Chinese sociologists in a symposium held under the auspices of the University of Chicago. Dr. Wu Ching-chao said on this occasion:

I think, we can get, say 20 to 30 per cent more of our population in the cities or in the small-sized towns, instead of crowding them all in the rural districts. . . . We hope to achieve that goal in about thirty years.[15]

[12] *The Chinese Year Book, 1940-41*, Council of International Affairs, Chungking, 1941, p. 45.

[13] *Planning Pamphlets*, National Planning Association, Washington D. C., No. 12, June, 1942, pp. 13, 14.

[14] *Foreign Affairs*, XXI, 3 (April, 1943), 491.

[15] Harley F. MacNair, ed., *Voices from Unoccupied China*, Chicago, 1944, p. xxix.

Dr. Fei Hsiao-t'ung asserted that the employment of larger numbers in transportation, manufacture, mines, and public works would have the effect of raising the standard of living of the farmers.[16] And Dr. Wu emphasized especially the social effects that could be expected from a greater vertical mobility in Chinese society.

Indeed, this aspect of our subject deserves more attention than it has yet received. As Sorokin has so well demonstrated, when a man remains throughout his life in the same occupational, economic, and political status, his behavior is dominated by inflexible habit; and this tends to acquire a traditional sanction when the position is fixed through generations. On the other hand, in a society that permits of occupational change, responses and reactions will vary; the more versatile who can easily adapt themselves to new situations will improve their position and, through their influence and example, give a new fluidity to the sense of values.[17] Of course, not every diversification of occupations has this result. In a caste-dominated society large technical and economic changes may take place without breaking down the established distances in social status. But economic modernization in China associates new occupations with the prestige conferred by participation in modern enterprise. Many stories are current of the sudden rise in the status of a man who has learned to drive a bus or to run an electric dynamo. On the other hand, a concentration of industry which creates backwaters of traditionalism in once-flourishing country towns has the effect of further reducing what little vertical mobility formerly existed in that type of community and of exaggerating stereotyped attitudes and modes of behavior.

Dr. Wu's reference to the smaller towns is especially to the point. The development of industry with foreign capital has made for an unhealthy concentration of manufacture in a few large cities and has helped to undermine the economic significance of the old centers of industry. These served a given region from which they took their raw materials and to which they offered a large variety of manufactured commodities. It is true,

[16] *Ibid.*, p. xxx.
[17] Pitirim Sorokin, *Social Mobility*, New York, 1927, Chapter XXI, "The Effects of Mobility on Human Behavior and Psychology."

there has always been some specialization, but with the undeveloped facilities of transportation before the era of railway
building this was secondary to the regional functioning of these
towns and cities. The effect of metropolitan concentration was
two-fold: it drained from the smaller places industrial skill and
enterprise and it brought the local industries into competition
with mass production. The writer had occasion to observe the
devastating influence of Shanghai's industrial growth on some
of the smaller industrial cities of Chekiang [18] and, in contrast, the
stimulating effect which the introduction of modern equipment
and modern organization had on the revival of a small industrial
town in Hopei.[19]

On the opposite side of the ledger are the decreased opportunities in the postwar period for the relief of population pressure in China through the employment of Chinese labor abroad,
and especially through emigration for continued residence
abroad. It is very doubtful that the gates of the dependent territories in Southeast Asia—not to speak of those in self-governing
countries or in the Dominions—will soon be opened again widely
to Chinese contract laborers or peasants in search of land.

With each installment of greater self-government, the social
and economic opportunities for Chinese immigrants in the now-
dependent countries of Southeast Asia will become less attractive. Nationality-conscious popular legislatures may be expected
even more than in the past to impede the easy path of clever
newcomers to influence and wealth. Restrictions against immigration are more likely to be increased than to be lessened. A
free China will probably be able to secure special agreements to
protect the rights acquired by Chinese nationals in these countries, but it will neither be strong enough nor desirous to force
upon them additional Chinese population. Generalissimo Chiang
Kai-shek made clear the intentions of the national government,

[18] See also the Introduction to D. K. Lieu's *The Growth and Industrialization of Shanghai,* Shanghai, 1936.

[19] H. D. Fong, *Rural Weaving and the Merchant Employers in a North
China District,* 80 pp.; *The Growth and Decline of Rural Industrial Enter-
prise in North China,* 82 pp.; Nos. 7 and 8 of Industry Series, Nankai
Institute of Economics, Tientsin, 1935 and 1936.

when in a message to the New York Herald Tribune Forum on Current Problems, delivered on November 17, 1942, he said:

Among our friends there has recently been some talk of China emerging as the leader of Asia, as if China wished the mantle of an unworthy Japan to fall on her shoulders. Having herself been victim of exploitation, China has infinite sympathy for the submerged nations of Asia, and toward them China feels she has only responsibilities—not rights. ... China has no desire to replace Western imperialism in Asia with an Oriental imperialism or isolationism of its own or of anyone else.[20]

The Chinese imperialism here disclaimed has at various times been said to be a reality not so much in the South as in the West and North. More recently it has taken the form of forecasts that the new developments of Chinese enterprise in Sinkiang will sooner or later collide in the Border Region with Russian interests. Such predictions seem to be based more on theory than on a gleaning from recent news reports. The westward migration of peasants from Kansu into Sinkiang is itself an illustration of the economic importance of political security: it was a spontaneous movement from agriculturally less to more advantageous areas following the pacification of a wild country previously infested with banditry and disturbed by civil war. It also illustrates competition for population between neighboring provinces: in recent years the flow of migrants, which owed its origin to efforts of the Sinkiang provincial government to attract settlers, has been reversed. The Kansu provincial government, thoroughly alarmed, took every means—such as the enforcement of tax claims—to prevent further migration and even to bring emigrants back. Even if Kansu, with a reform program as yet mostly on paper, should fail, there is no probability whatever of a large-scale Chinese emigration from Sinkiang into Siberian territory. Sinkiang itself, for the peasant accustomed to an intensive community life, is just about the end of his world. And in recent years this great Border Region has been discovered to be somewhat richer in natural resources than the forbidding appearance of much of it, including the Takla Makan Desert, had led earlier explorers to believe. With the new road communica-

[20] Chiang Kai-shek, *Resistance and Reconstruction,* New York, 1943, p. 317.

tions now planned and partly already in being, this enormous province may be able to absorb several million people. The Sinkiang provincial government showed itself eager to receive a large quota of Honan famine refugees, and some of these are reported to have reached this western outpost and to have taken up land there.

The part which Sinkiang plays as a potential recipient of Chinese population from more densely settled parts of China before it can flow beyond the national borders is also to some extent played by Ningshia. Only its resources apparently are much more modest. This province also adjoins Kansu, on its northern side. It has lost population (from one and a half million in 1933 to an estimated 720,000 in 1942) for reasons that have nothing to do with its capacity to support population. Under the governorship of General Ma Hungkwei, some progress has been made in improving conditions, but much land is left unreclaimed because the alkaline nature of the soil does not permit of exploitation by traditional methods.[21] There are permanent reasons why the coal reserves and other resources of this province have not been more fully exploited. The whole Moslem Northwest has for centuries suffered from neglect. From this region Chinese agricultural colonization at times extended into Outer Mongolia, without, however, being able to take very deep roots.

Ningshia itself, like Kansu, as recent surveys have shown, is capable of some irrigation for intensive agriculture, but especially of animal husbandry in a more concentrated form. Mongolia, quite apart from the intelligent desire of its leaders to develop the country for its own people and in keeping with its own semi-nomadic way of life, is much poorer in such opportunities. It would be difficult to think of reasons why either Chinese peasants or a strong Chinese national government should prefer colonization in Mongolia to a somewhat denser settlement of the northwestern provinces of China Proper. Moreover, such a movement could probably not take place without subsidies.

We are not here concerned with questions of disputed sovereignty. But any uncertainty in that respect would only be an

[21] *Chungyang Jih Pao,* November 13, 1942 (in Chinese).

additional reason why a flow of Chinese colonists into Outer Mongolia is not likely to happen in the years following the war, except possibly within the most modest limits in the wake of trade.[22] To think that any of the skill and enterprise developed overseas by South Chinese or transplanted during the present war from eastern to western China can be siphoned off into the inhospitable borderlands of the Northwest certainly is unrealistic. The fuller utilization of the natural resources in these marginal areas will be dictated by the industrial needs of Central China if not of China's creditors. There may be some intraregional redistribution of population; but a large flow of labor beyond the Great Wall is improbable.

Somewhat different, of course, is the case of the Manchurian Chinese who fled to China Proper after the Japanese occupation of Manchuria in 1932 and 1933, and who desire to return to their homes (see above, p. 88). Nor is it at all probable, once a reasonably good government has been installed at Hsinking or Mukden, that several million Chinese in Manchuria who still have links with their home communities below the Great Wall will either wish or be encouraged to return. From the standpoint of international investment as well as from that of China's own economic planning, it will be more advantageous to develop large-scale enterprises of many kinds in Manchuria rather than to repatriate masses of people to provinces already densely populated where droughts and floods still threaten their livelihood. It is true, a strong love of home characterizes these emigrants from Hopei and Shantung, but their movements have in the past been regulated somewhat by the reports received from the home communities, and this influence will still be strong. These provinces, under a modern type of development, could maintain their present populations on a much higher level of comfort and security. But that security involves also far-reaching reforms of local government, and especially of the system of taxation; and these reforms, to which the national government is pledged, cannot be accomplished in a few months. The funds needed for large reclamation projects are unlikely to be forthcoming until there is a guarantee of continued good government.

[22] The whole complicated situation is set forth by Owen Lattimore in *Inner Frontiers of China*, New York, 1940. See also above, p. 91.

The probability, therefore, is that after the enemy's defeat there will at first be a southward drift of people who have been kept far from home against their will. But the long-range flow of population will be in the opposite direction, to the great northern land of opportunity.[23]

It has been suggested that, with the closing of industrial opportunity for Chinese merchants in some of the countries of Southeast Asia, some of these enterprising men will take advantage of the national government's desire more fully to develop the incipient industries of the borderland, and that with government aid they will attempt to divert to that region part of the labor surplus of the crowded southeastern provinces which used to emigrate to the Nan Yang. For reasons already stated, it is improbable that such a movement will assume large proportions. But it might make, within narrow limits, a valuable contribution toward that greater horizontal mobility which in itself is highly to be desired. In this connection the climatically stimulating effect of even a temporary transference, under contract, of a labor force from the hot and humid coastal region to the dry interior should not be overlooked. For a population rich in skills but worn down by poverty and neglect this may prove a factor of importance.[24]

Such increased activity within China cannot suffice to offset the closed outlets of foreign emigration. But it need not do so entirely. For example, there is no reason why, under new treaty arrangements, considerable *temporary* movements of Chinese labor forces to and from the Nan Yang without the right of permanent settlement may not continue for a long time. Eventually, with improved speed of travel, there may, in fact, be new opportunities for seasonal labor migration to areas with fluctuating labor requirements.[25]

[23] The population of Manchuria, according to a Japanese estimate, has grown from about 30 million in the early 'thirties to 43 million in 1943.

[24] This suggestion comes from George B. Cressey (*Asia's Lands and Peoples*, New York, 1944, p. 168), who, however, warns that the possibilities of relief through redistribution of population from the crowded to the sparsely settled parts of China are, under present conditions of technology, definitely limited (*ibid.*, p. 44).

[25] For evidence of the valuable contributions made by Chinese labor to the economic development of Southeast Asia, see, in addition to the sources

The question is, can China afford to have millions of its young men place their energies at the service of foreign countries and of foreign capitalists? Even though some of their savings flow back home, these men, supported by the home soil in their unproductive years, contribute all too little to the wealth of China. The fault is not theirs. The same energy that has been dominant in the economic development of Malaya, Thailand, British Borneo, and the Philippines, would long ago have been applied to the homeland had conditions been halfway favorable. But, as has already been pointed out, in the past every promising beginning of such enterprise has sooner or later fallen victim to political disorders, to a weakness of local and provincial governments so great as to permit rampant banditry, to fluctuations in prices and currencies that have wiped out large fortunes, and to a general loss of those elementary safeguards on which an orderly conduct of industry and commerce depends. The home counties of Chinese emigrant communities are strewn with the wreckage of railway and bus lines, with factories dismantled, wharves and steamships rotting away, orchards abandoned, and other evidences of a futile struggle of modern enterprise against unfavorable conditions. Many of these undertakings were enormously profitable for a few years before the envy of a rival faction or the greed of a war lord destroyed them. In recent prewar years, with the national government more firmly in the saddle, Canton and Swatow and Amoy, even some of the smaller towns, began to assume the appearance of flourishing centers of modern industry. The ever-growing Japanese encroachments against which the government was powerless at the time destroyed these promising beginnings.

Above all, there is the question of what a determined program of agrarian reforms may do to stabilize the Chinese population. Historically there is ample justification for the belief that good government makes for a larger survival and, in an oriental setting, for larger families and a more rapid reproduction. But there are also present in the traditional mores incipient restraints that can be developed and implemented. As in Korea (see above,

already named, "The Chinese in Southeastern Asia and the Philippines," by Patricia G. Barnett, *Annals of the American Academy of Political and Social Science*, CCVI (March, 1943), 32-49.

p. 92, note 12), so certainly in China, too, the enormous cost of customary rites, especially of funerals and marriage celebrations,[26] and the sacred duty imposed upon children to support their parents, must be regarded as measures intended to counteract an excessive birth-rate; and there is reason to believe that these customs, as also the size of dowries and other matters of customary expense, have been regulated at times to keep reproduction within bounds. Although in China, as in all pre-industrial societies, an excessive human fertility has been countered through the ages by abortion, infanticide, and sale of children, voluntary restraint was not unknown. The concern with over-population goes back at least to the fourth century;[27] and it is known that the Emperor Chien Lung, a contemporary of Malthus, warned against it despite his pre-occupation with the recruitment of large armies.[28]

In the Chinese code of ethics, family survival is by no means the only obligation. Social continuity is, and can be, assured, as many stories show, by adoption in case of need. The essence of the code is that the experience of the group and the wisdom distilled from it shall not be lost. Not only the individual ancestor but the sage village magistrate, elevated to divine honors, is always present to admonish the living generation, so that its heritage may not diminish or be lost by foolish experiment. Only in times of trouble and unusual economic uncertainty does the possession of many sons become an insurance that worship of the ancestors will continue uninterrupted; and since the prosperous will have more sons than the poor, the large family assumes a symbolic quality of prestige and tends to become an end in itself for which men will sacrifice other comforts.

Recent social studies show that the basic core of Chinese ethics persists but that, under a variety of circumstances, a rapidly growing sector of Chinese society is abandoning the

[26] See Sidney D. Gamble, *How Chinese Families Live in Peiping*, New York, 1933, Chapter X; Ta Chen, *Emigrant Communities in South China*, New York, 1940, p. 136; J. Lossing Buck, *Land Utilization in China*, Chicago, 1937, pp. 467-70.

[27] Herbert D. Lamson, *op. cit.*, p. 557.

[28] C. G. Dittmer, "Density of Population and the Standard of Living in North China," *Publications of the American Sociological Society*, XIX (1925), 196 (quoted by Lamson).

prestige value of the large family for values more in keeping with the moral implications of good citizenship and personal success.[29] The introduction of birth-control clinics in China would be futile, indeed, if there were not already a widespread demand for the knowledge and implements which they dispense.

Those young Chinese who have gone forth to labor abroad have remained peasants in their attitudes, for the most part. Moreover, it has been customary for them to insure offspring at home, either by a very early marriage before leaving or through occasional visits home for the special purpose of procreation, even when they had founded another family overseas.[30] There is no reason to believe, therefore, that an absorption in the future of a large proportion of this landless proletariat in non-agricultural occupations at home would represent a corresponding additional pressure of population in South China. Under moderately favorable conditions the changes in China's internal economy, already indicated above, should suffice to make up for a reduced volume of emigration.

12

POSTWAR PROSPECTS IN JAPAN

FEAR OF A LARGE JAPANESE EMIGRATION is likely to revive when, after military defeat, the empire will face a world of greatly diminished opportunities for economic expansion. It may therefore be well to add a brief indication of the population trends as shown by the last census and other population statistics. Whether a marked decrease of the excess of male over female population in 1940 as compared with 1935—17,712 in a total population of 73,114,308 as against 214,118 in a total population of 69,254,148—has a significance other than as a characteristic

[29] Much documentary evidence will be found in a study of the Chinese family by Olga Lang, soon to be published.
[30] See Ta Chen, *Emigrant Communities*, p. 140.

war-time phenomenon is doubtful. Of unquestionable importance, on the other hand, is a decline in population increase
from 7.9 per cent in 1925-30 and 7.5 per cent in 1930-35 to only
5.6 per cent in 1935-40. Although there was no marked decrease
in the number of women in the reproductive age group, large-
scale mobilization produced an immediate effect on the birth-
rate in the war years 1938-40. But the decline in population
growth reflects only in part a falling birth-rate, the lowest since
1919 despite all the government could do to encourage large
families.[1] It also reflects a rise in the death-rate which in 1938
was the highest on record since 1929 and may have further
increased since then.

A comparison by age groups shows that, apart from an infantile mortality which is from two to almost five times as high
as in other industrial countries, the excess of deaths over those
in other countries occurs mainly in the years of adolescence and
early adulthood (not counting those killed in war).[2] This means
that the growth of the Japanese population is impeded more
especially by the strains of the country's economy on the reproductive age group. Whether that strain makes itself felt more
by morbidity and mortality or by voluntary birth control does
not affect the net result. The rising marriage age for both
sexes, more in particular that of women, points to a continuation
of voluntary birth control. War, of course, unless long continued, may mean merely deferred marriage, and too much
should not be made of a decrease in the number of marriages
between 1937 and 1938 by 17 per cent. However, the divorce
rate is rising and, though not yet significant numerically, points
to the effect on married life of urbanization rather than of war.
Between 1930 and 1940, the proportion of the rural population
in the total decreased from 69.5 to 62.3 per cent; and this is
probably the most far-reaching symptom of a change likely to
continue into peace times.

A Chinese commentator[3] concludes from these and other

---

[1] Reduction of taxes for large families, loans, increased restriction on
female employment, educational propaganda.

[2] For an estimate of the military losses of Japan, see *Metropolitan Life
Insurance Bulletin*, XXIV, 1 (January, 1943).

[3] In *War-Time Japan*, July 1, 1941, in Chinese.

recent figures (such as those here given on p. 50 *et seq.*) that the population of Japan Proper, as distinct from Greater Japan, is becoming exhausted by a war effort which began even before 1937, and that "the decrease of Japanese population is not only a temporary tendency but also limits its future development." A comparison of the available data would suggest, rather, that with the frugality and high traditional birth-rate of the Japanese people the direct demographic effects of the war might perhaps under favorable postwar conditions be overcome in a single generation. From the standpoint of world population policy the long-range effects of Japan's recent economic and social history are more important. There are indications that the anachronism of an oriental peasant demography in a country that is becoming rapidly industrialized is nearing its end. The same influences that have slowed down population growth in other technically advanced countries, and in some of them have produced an actual decline, have been at work in Japan for some time, have become accentuated under war conditions, and must be expected still to operative under whatever peace terms may be imposed upon the empire.[4] This view seems to be shared by Professor Steiner. After reviewing recent trends and the probable effects of the war, he says:

When all these facts are taken into consideration, it would seem safe to conclude that Japan's period of swarming has definitely ended and may be succeeded by a period of actual population decline in the near future.[5]

In all such forecasts intangible psychological factors are involved which it is especially difficult to appraise in the case of a people like the Japanese, of whose mental processes, despite a prodigious amount of writing on the subject, Occidentals are singularly ill informed. If the Japanese react to their defeat, as some predict, with a mood of utter dejection, it is possible that their marriage- and birth-rates will decline at a precipitous rate. If, on the other hand, their empire-centered religious faith remains

[4] See Allen B. Cole, "Japan's Population Problems in War and Peace," *Pacific Affairs*, XVI, 4 (December, 1943) 397-417.

[5] Jesse F. Steiner, "Population Trends in Japan," *American Sociological Review*, IX, (February, 1944), 38.

and they throw themselves with patriotic fervor into a national discipline dominated by a desire for future reassertion and revenge, then heroic feats in human breeding must be expected, and an increase in numbers wholly unrelated to the country's ability to support them. Something of this sort happened at the beginning of the Meiji Era, though under a somewhat different stimulus: the sense of freedom from the feudal shackles suffered during the two and a half centuries of the Tokugawa regime. Relief from oppression was not, of course, the only impetus to procreation, though it is true that:

> Personal freedom and economic opportunity swept away the controls which had formerly kept the population static, and, in the early days of the Emperor Meiji's reign, the government set about reducing the death rate of infants and aged people.[6]

There was also the constructive design of the new government to convert the Japanese Isles as quickly as possible into an arsenal and a super-plant of modern industry.

But leaving aside the early years of the new regime when census procedures may not have been altogether reliable, it is interesting to note that the rate of population growth in the four decades of emancipation, 1880 to 1900, was less than that in the next four decades of increased industrialization and urbanization, namely, 34.2 as against 41.0 per cent. The birth-rate did not begin to decline until about 1920, but in the following two decades the age composition, because of the preceding rapid growth of the population, still was such as to make for a high rate of reproduction. Industrialization and urbanization were accomplished with a population which in social attitudes and standards of living still was largely rural. Concentration of the population, and especially the modern provisions of public health in the large cities, helped to reduce death-rates; but there was not yet that penetration of modern ideas which makes for individualism and smaller families. This, of course, is partly to be attributed to the deliberate policy of a government which, long before even the war with China, used every device to

[6] Guy-Harold Smith and Dorothy Good, *Japan, a Geographical View*, New York, 1943, p. 48.

impress upon the people the first duty of citizenship: to bring into life sons who might carry arms in defense of the emperor.

Pessimists point out that, even with a decreased birth-rate, the present age and sex composition of the population makes inevitable a substantial growth, a growth much too large for easy absorption in a time of economic reconstruction and re-orientation. To provide outlets for that additional population is just as much a task for United Nations peace-time strategy, they say, as it is to provide safeguards against a possible Japanese re-armament.[7] Some Americans frankly advocate that, at whatever cost to our standard of living, we must outbreed the Japanese.[8] Others, the great majority, see no contradiction in a proposed United Nations policy which would (a) liberally provide for Japan's peaceful economic expansion through access to raw materials and trade opportunities but (b) abstain from any interference—other than that necessitated by the desire to prevent re-armament—with that country's internal affairs.[9] Obviously, with such a policy toward Japan that country's re-adoption of a policy of stimulated population growth for aggressive national ends would be merely a question of time. If that were the case, the world would before long confront large demands, not only from Japanese militarists, but also from liberals with a high sense of social responsibility, for concessions to ease the empire's problem of overpopulation. And these demands, at a time of growing nationalism among colored peoples everywhere, may combine with those of other oriental peoples to produce the tinder for a war between races.

With the loss of Manchuria, of Korea, and of all the island possessions, with the collapse of the expanded empire and the uncertainty of almost every prop in Japan's future economic structure, no curve drawn from the population statistics of the past affords reliable guidance to future probabilities. Some of the two and a half million Japanese living abroad probably will

[7] The "Japan" number of *Fortune*, April, 1944, raises this problem but does not answer it.

[8] See, for example, Mark Sullivan's syndicated article in the *New York Herald Tribune* for March 31, 1944, p. 21.

[9] This seems to be among the conclusions separately arrived at by several round tables of more or less well-informed Americans lately held under the auspices of the American Council of the Institute of Pacific Relations.

return to the homeland, but not necessarily all, or even a majority. Japan will be more dependent than ever on imported food, and that food will be supplied in the main by such countries as Burma and Indo-China which do not disdain to receive Japanese manufactures in exchange, and in which industrialization, though desired, is not likely to make very rapid progress. With other possibilities of secure foreign trade, with changed consumer demands and standards of living in the Japanese homeland, with a more intensive utilization of the marginal cultivable areas, with increased mobility and urbanization, perhaps with domestic social and educational policies expressive of a more democratic regime, and with other influences too numerous to mention and too complex to evaluate, we do not know whether enough forces may not be set to work to keep the growth of the empire's population under control. No one can tell today exactly what combination of forces will bring this about.

In view of the sharp divergences of opinion as to the causes of differential birth-rates as between East and West, rural and urban populations, China and Japan, etc., the question of social motivation in given circumstances deserves closer consideration. To begin with, recent studies of an intensive character anywhere have thrown some doubt on purely biological explanations which at one time were far more current. The very term "fertility" when applied to the actual birth-rate per thousand women of child-bearing age in different places and regions has to be defined in general rather than biological terms; for, the statistician does not know at what point the effects of "fertility" in the true sense merge into those of environmental causes. In most recent studies the term is understood in its newer connotations, including the net result of all influences that determine the birth-rate, and taking it for granted that variations in motivation, including the effects of outside pressures, are more important factors than possible divergences in physiological determinants.

Thus Allan B. Cole, in a rational analysis of Japan's declining birth-rate,[10] mentions first the indisputable fact that "demographic expansion" after the people's liberation from feudal fetters has made possible the development of industry and urbani-

10 *Op. cit.*, p. 403.

137

zation, not *vice versa*. The rising plane of living, particularly in cities, induces persons of limited means to marry later and have fewer children.

There is no convincing evidence that urban capacity to reproduce has been depressed in Japan: rather it is obvious that deliberate private birth control has been increasing for years.

But the urban environment does not possess some mystic quality which operates automatically. Its effect on social attitudes can be discovered through observation. Cole draws attention to the fact, for example, that in Japanese industry there is far more artificial segregation of the sexes than in the countryside. One might add that institutionalized prostitution also is especially characteristic of Japanese towns and cities; the lack of social intercourse between men and women outside (and to some extent also within) the family circle holds down the illegitimate birth-rate and has a lowering effect on the legitimate birth-rate, too. The industries drawing man power from the villages, moreover, are to some extent concentrated in different cities from those drawing woman power; and in the latter the provisions of dormitories in prison-like compounds is customary. In the cities the Japanese worker comes in contact with new ideas. Even though he may not absorb any particular social "ideology," nevertheless some new personal purposes are liable to take root and old ones, always taken for granted in the traditional village society—including the absolute desirability of multitudinous offspring—become sufficiently doubted no longer to dominate actions and habits.

Birth control as an educational movement has had its ups and downs in Japan. At the beginning of this century it was introduced by liberal and radical groups along with other Western ideas. It spread rapidly in the 'twenties when it received considerable support from the government as a means of raising prosperity. A few years later, however, a government less friendly to liberal social policies took alarm and, with other measures to stimulate a larger birth-rate, actively prevented the spread of birth-control information. Furthermore, in Japan especially, children are more difficult to bring up in cities and urban districts than in the agricultural village. While earnings are higher, the village-born parents will be more impressed by the high cost of living. It is not really difficult to reconstruct the thoughts of the village-born mother when she has already brought two or three children into the world.

Although the determined leadership in "movements" has belonged largely to the rebellious middle-class women who had time, education, money and social backing for their reforms, a combative spirit has manifested itself elsewhere, too, among mill operatives and farmers' wives....

The peasant woman, overburdened with family, working in the fields as well as in extra-seasonal occupations indoors, such as basket-weaving, leads so severe, so isolated and so exhausting a life that young girls turn to the mills and the city offices as a refuge.[11]

The higher plane of living in the cities, already referred to, is of course the most important factor. Several recent writers use the term "feminization" in describing the changes that have taken place in the consuming habits of Japanese city dwellers: women have been affected by, or instrumental in, these changes much more than men. They demand things the very use of which their mothers or grandmothers would not have understood and for which even the higher earnings in urban occupations would be wholly insufficient if the homes were filled with children.

Overpopulation in Japan, then, is primarily rural overpopulation. And even this is unequally distributed. Contrary to popular belief, a minute subdivision of the cultivable land does not necessarily make for the most intensive possible agricultural production. Modern techniques with the use of improved implements and power-driven machinery have thus far been introduced, as is but natural, more in the processing of agricultural products than in agriculture itself. We have no reason to believe that mechanization of agriculture would have the same effect on social attitudes as the growth of urban industries which involves much greater changes in habits; but it is probable that any deviation from traditional farming methods would have significant psychological by-products. There has been much discussion in Japan of rural industrialization as a means of providing fuller

[11] Miriam Beard, *Realism in Romantic Japan*, New York, 1930, pp. 181, 194. See also Jesse F. Steiner, *Behind the Japanese Mask*, New York, 1943, Chapter vi.

employment for the farm population;[12] but the problem has usually been stated as though solely relating to the introduction of small industries for the local utilization of agricultural products, not as relating also and perhaps principally to the processes of agricultural production itself.

There was, in fact, a five-year plan for the reconstruction of rural life, from 1932 to 1937, on the theory that an effective improvement in agricultural production could come only from a community-centered movement relating new techniques and new forms of organization, new forms of credit and of marketing to a central social concern with the improvement of living conditions.[13] Unfortunately, the movement soon became absorbed in that expanionist and militarist patriotic movement of which the young men's associations in the villages were the principal carriers, and of which the ever-increasing controls of the central government in the interest of war-time food supplies was the eventual death. Nevertheless, the plan was essentially sound and, with a more democratic orientation, carries promise for the future.

13

POSTWAR PROSPECTS IN KOREA

UNDER A SOUND REGIME in the interest of the Korean people, they too would undergo economic developments sufficient to eliminate the need for any large-scale emigration for some time to come. Korean overseas migration never has amounted to much, either under the old national government or under Japanese domination. The obvious outlets of surplus population were—and continue to be—to Manchuria and the Maritime Territory

[12] *E.g.*, Shiroshi Nasu, *Aspects of Japanese Agriculture*, New York, 1941, Chapter XI, "Land Utilization and Population."

[13] Shiroshi Nasu, "Ziele und Ausrichtung der Japanischen Agrarpolitik in der Gegenwart," *Weltwirtschaftliches Archiv*, XLVI, 1 (July, 1937), 157-84.

of Siberia, but there is no immediate probability of a large movement for permanent settlement in either direction. Even with a considerable return migration of Koreans from Japan, the development of Korean commercial agriculture and industry in the days of reconstruction may suffice to create employment comparable in extent with that formerly found in Japan. At the time of writing there is a labor shortage in Korea. This, of course, was induced by the necessity of intensifying the production of war materials in Korea at the same time that large numbers of workers were drawn off to man the Japanese war industries in Manchuria and Japan Proper. Before the war is over there may be a million and a half or two million Koreans in Japan, large numbers of whom will wish to return to their homeland. In this connection it should be remembered, however, that the return migration from Japan to Korea has always been substantial,[1] and that Korean industries for home consumption have been starved during the Japanese regime, so that even a relatively mild revival would be capable of employing a large proportion of the returned emigrants.[2] There are, then, two possibilities: If Korea should continue to be economically geared to Japanese industry, Korean labor, as that of the docile and underpaid bottom class, would certainly be used by Japanese capitalists even if this were to involve a further growth of industrial plants in Korea at the expense of that in Japan. If Korea is freed and receives the benefit of adequate foreign investments without conditions of unfreedom, the opportunity for the employment of Korean labor at home will be better than

[1] Of 1,186,000 Koreans who entered Japan between 1917 and 1929, only about 338,000 remained permanently. *International Labour Review*, December, 1930.

[2] In the fifteen years 1922 to 1937, the number of workers in Korean industry increased from 46,000 to 207,000; in the one year 1937-38 it increased by another 24,000. But even in 1938, when Koreans formed about one-third of the population of Greater Japan, the number of industrial employees in Korea was only 7.2 per cent of those in Japan Proper—a clear sign that the country is industrially under-developed and almost entirely dependent on Japan for its manufactured consumer goods. Korea's "progress," in fact, shows all the elements of a purely colonial economy, with one-fourth of the industrial production—even in the war year 1938—contributed by household industry. (Andrew J. Grajdanzev, *Modern Korea*, New York, 1944.)

it has been since the turn of the century. With its excellent natural resources and with its industrious working population, Korea would be able to leap into the modern world of mass production and international exchange.

Looking to a more distant future, the prospect for Korea is less clear. The economic spurt following upon liberation may, as intimated above, absorb the immediate population surplus resulting from the return of emigrants. But it could hardly be expected to keep pace with the Korean birth-rate unless this were to diminish considerably or other influences came into play.[3] Between 1925, when the first modern population census was taken, and 1940, the population increased by one-fourth. The first effect of economic improvement, in a population three-fourths agricultural and more than 90 per cent rural, will be to decrease the death-rate. A corresponding or larger decrease of the birth-rate is unlikely to take place unless there should occur a revolutionary change in social attitudes. In 1938, only 2.6 per cent of the population was engaged in industry. Even if we add to this the proportions engaged in other non-agricultural pursuits and expect the relative importance of all of these in the total population to double in a generation, the people would still be a preponderately rural one. With a population density of about 500 per square mile in the more intensively cultivated southern provinces, it is improbable that further improvements in agriculture will contribute much to absorb the natural growth of the population. Only very large capital investments in the naturally poorer northern provinces would make this possible, and even there the population density is relatively high: about 200 per square mile.

Overpopulation in Korea as in other eastern Asiatic countries

[3] The average density of population is only 268 per square mile as compared with one of 495 in Japan, but the population is very unevenly distributed, varying from 119 persons per square mile in North Kankyo Province to 525 in Keiki Province (which contains the capital, Seoul). The movement of laborers from the purely rural South to the North, already referred to, has assumed a new impetus from the growth of new centers of industry, Seishin, Heijo, and others. Although the growth of population is dangerously rapid, foreign experts believe that, even with only a moderate program of industrialization, Korea could export about one-fifth of its rice production without suffering a shortage of food.

is bound to occur under conditions favorable to survival unless the birth-rate itself declines. And this is not likely to take place except with a considerable change in the country's economy and way of living. It is sometimes pointed out that Korea has not the same advantages for industrialization as its neighbors: neither the great mineral resources of Manchuria nor the advanced technical development of Japan. But it does have special advantages of its own. Korea is especially rich in actual and potential water power. It is close enough to the Manchurian resources and to overseas markets to fill some of the functions of secondary industry between primary production and manufacture of consumer goods. Nor are its own resources of industrial raw materials negligible. Before the Japanese conquest, Koreans were experienced fishermen; and the seas surrounding the peninsula teemed with life.[4] Reforestation of considerable areas not far from serviceable ports will produce timber that can be worked up, with the aid of water power, into semi-manufactured export commodities. Korea is far better equipped than China with means of transportation, and these have been developed by the Japanese to aid industry and export trade. Some parts of northern Korea are suitable for intensified pasturage under proper safeguards to conserve the soil; and although this will not absorb much man power, it may offer yet other materials for manufacture. In a large part of Korea agricultural work is seasonal, and this is one of the great causes of underemployment and poverty until auxiliary small industries are developed. In that development a well-designed distribution of electric power will perhaps play its most useful role.

In short, the prospects of a varied industrialization adapted to the special opportunities which Korea affords are quite good—assuming always that there will be access to foreign markets on equal terms with that of other countries and some protection against the dumping of foreign, specifically Japanese, manufactured goods on the internal market. Korean economists lay spe-

---

[4] An immediate difficulty on re-occupation will be to supply the Korean fishing industry with boats since practically all small craft has been commandeered by the Japanese. Korea depends on fish not only as a major source of food protein but also as fertilizer.

cial stress on the development of the village and small-town crafts into industries utilizing to the full the existing skills of the people. They point out that the proportion of Koreans engaged in skilled labor is much larger than the official reports would lead one to believe, because Korean workers in Japanese-dominated enterprises have deliberately been held down to a lower wage classification than Japanese engaged in similar work. They also point out that anti-Occidental prejudice hardly exists in Korea and that a rapid advance in industrialization is possible with the aid of foreign hydraulic engineers, mining and railroad experts, technicians and trade teachers.[5] Moreover, it should be remembered that for a generation the accumulation of capital by Koreans has been frustrated, but the Koreans are an industrious and thrifty people. With the proper stimuli and with suitable credit institutions, they will not for long have to depend for a program of industrialization entirely on foreign capital. And with industrialization there will come in Korea, as elsewhere, new social conditions, attitudes, and habits predisposing to birth control.

Opportunities for emigration, though they can only serve as a temporary easing of the population pressure, will be important in the period of transition. At least one such opportunity exists. In Tsarist days, Korean settlers introduced the cultivation of rice north of Vladivostok, and their success as colonizers was at times much appreciated.[6] Under Soviet rule, Korean immigration was discouraged, and large numbers of Korean settlers were expelled. They were regarded, and to some extent were, spearheads of Japanese expansion. But the climate and the soil of the Soviet Maritime Territory have not changed. The former, modified by the Pacific monsoons, probably still makes that region the most suitable in all the Soviet Union for the cultivation of rice. With its enormous program of economic reconstruction the Union may well resume the use of the attested skill of oriental peasants for the intensive cultivation of that region and employ European Russians on other tasks. While Koreans have done even better

[5] The population census of 1940 revealed the presence of only 1,500 Europeans in Korea.

[6] See above, p. 95.

in this respect in southern Manchuria, they will be less welcome there. Only time can heal the enmity which the manchinations of the Japanese masters has created between Manchurian Chinese and Koreans.

14

POSTWAR PROSPECTS IN SOUTHEAST ASIA

OVERPOPULATION, the pressure on resources which drives people from the land and creates a promising opening for the labor recruiter from distant lands, nearly always is localized. Centers of such pressure may be expected to exist after the war in Java, in the Philippines, in Indo-China. In our brief survey we have found no reason for doubting that whatever population "surpluses" may occur in these countries can readily be absorbed in the Asiatic tropics themselves. For example, the Netherlands Indian authorities are greatly concerned about the Javanese proletarian who owns no land and is liable to be crowded out of wage employment in times of economic depression. He is so much of a potential asset for Indonesia itself that even the settlement of larger numbers of Javanese in neighboring Malaya is regarded as less desirable than the increased use of Javanese labor to open up the insufficiently used resources of the Outer Islands for the benefit of Indonesia itself.

In the plans for the economic reconstruction of the Netherlands Indies, the full absorption of the working population is a fundamental aim. The labor needs of part of Sumatra, Borneo, and New Guinea under a systematically applied plan of development may be greater than can as yet be stated with certainty, though land utilization is limited over a large part by lack of natural fertility. However, above all the authorities count on all-around intensification of production and the growth of industry as the foremost means to lessen population pressure and

145

want.[1] Dr. Pelzer, after a thorough study of settlement possibilities, expresses the opinion that "agricultural colonization, although it cannot go on indefinitely, will nevertheless be able to take care of the population increase of Java and Madura for many decades."[2] Industrialization, he realizes, may have more far-reaching effects through its influence on living habits and social attitudes, but just now its possibilities, great as they are, will be likely to reach their saturation point more quickly than those of resettlement:

During the first years after the war industrialization will probably again be in the lead, but, I believe, only for a limited period. Once the development of secondary industries has reached a certain level, colonization may come to the forefront.... Natural resources and other requirements for the development of primary industries are lacking.

If this were the whole truth and all that can be seen ahead for the Netherlands Indies, and for Java in particular, the outlook would be bleak indeed—provided we accept the view current among so many students of population problems that industrialization and urbanization alone afford the opportunity for bringing influences to bear on an old oriental society making for a changed attitude toward large families and for voluntary birth control. This view the present author is not alone in regarding as incorrect.[3]

Does Malaya need Javanese labor? That dependency, politically and economically, has an uncertain future. It is conceivable that the partly joint administration with Sumatra, set up by the Japanese, will have proved so beneficial as to lead to some kind of British-Netherlands condominium, so as to apply common policies to the many problems which the two dependencies have in common. With an average population density of only 82

---

[1] J. H. Boeke, *The Structure of Netherlands Indian Economy*, New York, 1942, Chapter XV, "The Population Problem in Connection with Native Agriculture"; Jan O. M. Broek, *The Economic Development of the Netherlands Indies*, New York, 1942, Chapter VIII, "Post-War Prospects."

[2] *Pioneering in the Asiatic Tropics, in press*, Chapter VIII.

[3] See Raymond Kennedy, *The Ageless Indies*, New York, 1942, pp. 196-7.

persons per square mile,[4] or a little more if the states ceded to Thailand by Japan should be permanently lost, as compared with 817 persons in Java and Madura (1930), Malaya certainly is not overpopulated. But this assumes a continuing world market for the dependency's major export commodities, especially rubber,[5] or the reclamation of large jungle areas for food production. Another possibility would be the development of considerable areas for the growth of tropical export commodities that do not as yet loom large but are called for by new industrial techniques, and this in conjunction with a greater food production for self-sufficiency.[6]

There are in Malaya also unrealized possibilities of industrialization which may be more rapidly advanced under a colonial policy firmly focused upon the welfare of the native people. Several small-scale industries have been introduced by the Japanese to make up for the war-time loss of imports. Three new highways crossing the peninsula have been built and other roads improved. The great need is for technical knowledge and skills, and for the development or supplementation of the trade school at Kuala Lumpur which has graduated all too few Malays of the requisite technical ability. Of course, if all labor immigration were stopped Malaya could easily become self-sufficient in food, and its development might be arrested. But that is not at all likely to be the policy; indeed, it is more probable that the total world demand for rubber after the war will give the Malayan industry a new lease of life until the production of synthetic rubber becomes far cheaper than it is today.[7]

In Burma, likewise, many intangible factors enter into any reasonable forecast of population trends. There is little probability that the country will soon see a great industrial develop-

[4] Total population 4,385,000, census of 1931. In 1941, the population was estimated to be 5,561,000, composed of 2,316,000 Malays, 2,388,000 Chinese, 745,500 Indians, the rest Europeans, Eurasians, and others. (*Federated Malay States Government Gazette*, September 11, 1941.)

[5] See below, p. 177.

[6] British Malaya has not been self-sufficient even in the supply of fish, although the fishermen of the state of Kelantan, now ceded to Thailand, are famous for their skill and have supplied part of the peninsula's requirements.

[7] Under the Japanese regime rubber plantings have been extended.

ment other than along lines already well established. If Burma should soon achieve some form of political independence, however, the old animosity against India may flare up into a popular demand for greater self-sufficiency in manufactured consumer goods and the adoption of tariffs and other measures to make this possible. Deposits of minerals not now known to be present in any quantity may yet be discovered in Upper Burma, but with the lack of suitable coal and iron for steel manufacture there is little chance that these minerals can be used in the country itself to build up those basic industries which nowadays every nation desires. The Burmans have shown themselves thoroughly capable of utilizing their major agricultural resource, the fertile and water-rich level lands with their abundant crops of rice. There has never been any need, even from the standpoint of the foreign capitalist, to look outside of Burma for a sufficient supply of agricultural labor. In recent decades, the Kachin and other native minorities in the uplands of Burma, too, have been found thoroughly capable of adaptation to the growing of the great variety of food and industrial crops of which those drier lands are capable.

Therefore, while Burma need not yet anxiously look to the time when its natural resources will prove insufficient to feed the ever-growing population, there is, on the other hand, no reason, from the standpoint of the welfare of the people who now live in that favored land, why large numbers of aliens should be allowed to encroach upon their resources. Not even the modest industrial growth which seems to be in keeping with the reasonable aspirations of the Burmese requires the presence of alien workers in large numbers. Many crafts now represented among the Burmese people themselves are capable of rationalization and a degre of mechanization sufficient to permit of competition with the more highly developed export industries of India and Japan, and this on economically valid grounds and not only those of national pride.

The Burmese population has thus far (July, 1944) been little disturbed by the fortunes of war. The sources of their economic strength lie in agriculture and in village crafts not easily bombed out of existence. The lack of imports will have given greater impetus to intensification and specialization in food production

148

and in the small industries. The cultural homogeneity of the Burmese as consumers will have been strengthened. There will thus be economic and cultural elements added to the old political feud with India to make a resumption of Indian immigration highly unpopular. And under Japanese tuition enough Burmans will have been strengthened in their desire for their country's political autonomy not easily to permit an interference with their own interest, as they see it, on the part of a government in which they are not represented. Though there is not the same degree of hostility toward the Chinese as there is toward the Indians, this also applies to any possible large-scale Chinese immigration. Fortunately, both the Indian and the Chinese governments are entirely aware of the psychological dynamite that has accumulated in Burma and will respect any restrictions that are not discriminatory and permit a continuance of those commercial relations with Burma in which they are far more interested than in competition for its land and jobs.

In the Philippines the situation is similar to that in the Netherlands Indies. The Commonwealth government has on many occasions indicated its wish to utilize all its available labor forces to bring more of the undeveloped areas of the Islands under cultivation and to intensify production in areas already settled.[8] Here, as in the Netherlands Indies, experiments in the shift of population from crowded sections to new settlements on virgin soil have gone far enough to warrant the investment of large sums in great projects of forest clearance, land reclamation, and commercial agriculture. It would be difficult at this time to imagine a desire on the part of large masses of Javanese or Filipinos to go off to some country with a nontropical climate, other

[8] The National Land Settlement Act of January 3, 1938, contains in its preamble this statement of object: "to afford opportunity to own farms to tenant farmers and small farmers from congested areas . . . ; to encourage migration to sparsely populated regions and facilitate the amalgamation of the people in different sections of the Philippines." The Secretary of the Interior, Rafael Alunan, in an address on March 20, 1941, referred to the act, and the development plan based on it, as designed to serve the more equitable distribution of the population, the increase of agricultural productivity, and also in a larger sense the solution of the country's outstanding economic problems.

than perhaps for temporary opportunities of wage-labor under short contracts and with a certainty of ability to return home.[9]

Interestingly enough, it was emigration—to Hawaii and continental United States—which stimulated the movement for an orderly resettlement in the Philippine Islands themselves. There had long been a spontaneous migration, especially on the island of Luzon, from the most densely populated to less crowded areas; but the lack of transit facilities and the cultural distance between different population groups, a result of geographical separation, had impeded this natural flow. It required the experience of orderly methods of recruitment for contract labor at a distance to lay the foundation for government-directed projects of resettlement at home. The Philippine Independence Act has stopped further emigration to the United States and to Hawaii. Thousands of laborers have been repatriated and, with their savings, have at least been able better to meet the economic problems of their own families.

The postwar prospects for Indo-China, as has already been intimated (p. 27), can hardly as yet be clearly distinguished. With population estimates based on an unreliable census taken more than twenty years ago, with the temporary alienation of important territories, with a flight of population of unknown proportions, with partly realized plans to transfer population from north to south, and with a clouded political outlook, any prognostication must of necessity be a hesitant one. Persons familiar with Indo-China point out that the great majority of peasants probably have been little affected by the war: their production has been largely for home consumption, they

[9] In this connection the writer wishes to throw out the suggestion that, in the interest of a more rapid internal economic development and social advance, it may be desirable to provide quite large numbers of young men in tropical and subtropical Asia with the opportunity of working for a few years abroad during early manhood. There is no doubt that the climatic change, under proper safeguards, would be physically stimulating. Even though engaged in manual labor, most of the migrants would receive valuable mental stimulants and incentives to further education. The socially and politically dangerous limitation of foreign contacts to members of the wealthy classes would give way to a broader participation of the people in the adaptation of their habits and customs to modern world conditions. See also below, p. 186.

have always been too poor to buy imported or other manufactured goods; and if some of them have shifted to slightly more primitive methods of making a living, they will under favorable circumstances soon regain at least their former standards. Favorable also is the improvement and extension of the road system, even though not all the new construction for military purposes will be suited to serve those of trade, and the new rail connections with Burma and Malaya may be of no help to the Indo-Chinese farmer. On the other hand, a considerable increase of phosphate and chrome mining to meet Japanese military needs may give the colony a continuing addition of potential export commodities.

It is to be feared, nevertheless, that with nine-tenths of its population engaged in agriculture, Indo-China will for long remain dependent for its prosperity on the world price of its one great export commodity, rice. The beginnings of industry are too small and too devoid of possibilities of rapid expansion to promise relief for the ever-growing pressure of population on the land. Only measures which are now outside the scope of practical politics—as, for example, a more preferred position for Indo-Chinese products on the French market than the French people were willing to accede to them before the war—would make the lot of the Indo-Chinese people tolerably secure. In the longer run, there can be no remedy for a growth of population which apparently—we have no exact figures—exceeds all bounds of prudence.

Thailand, with all its economic and political problems, does not figure among those countries of eastern Asia plagued by a population problem in which external migration can play an important part. Of its 6,824,000 people whose occupations are recorded, 6,029,000 are engaged in agriculture, according to the 1937 census report. Even without the new accessions of territory, which may be lost again, the country has a sufficient cultivable area to meet the needs of its people for a long time to come, and this especially if some of its prewar government's excellent plans for intensified production and for modernization of living conditions should mature. There is, however, in Thailand the same maldistribution of population which is common to the rice-producing countries of the monsoon region. People are crowded together on low-lying, humid plains—especially the Menam Valley—to produce export crops when, with better tools, enterprising leadership, and a more far-sighted policy of capital investment, they could spread out over a much larger cultivable area—with great benefit to their health and happiness though perhaps with a slightly less "favorable" balance of foreign trade.

PART V

EMIGRATION BEYOND ASIA

15

PROSPECTS AND POLICIES

The Role of Oriental Labor

AT MORE THAN ONE POINT in the preceding chapters, what started out as a study of migration movements in eastern Asia expanded of necessity to take in a larger view. For many centuries the region has received an influx of population from other parts of the world; but this has never amounted to more than a fraction of the migratory stream of which it was the source. Even if there were no fear of a world-inundation with Asiatic surplus population, the probabilities of postwar migration and resettlement within eastern Asia could not be realistically indicated without taking into account emigration movements, past and present, that go far outside the framework of the region's inner readjustments. To arrive at the basic elements of a world policy, population strategists will have to consider carefully the prospects of a resumption, and possibly enlargement, of that international migration which has in the past distributed millions of Asiatics over non-Asiatic lands. It is true, in the meantime world opinion under the influence of organized labor has become hostile to the use of cheap oriental labor as a means of economic development in countries where occidental farmers and wage-earners must earn a living. But there has also been a growth in the influence of oriental peoples on world politics, and the white man may not be able for much longer to control the settlement and uses of the world's less densely populated territories in opposition to the wishes of crowded Asiatic peoples. These have become politically awakened. Many of their spokesmen are convinced that in other parts of the world there are areas well suited for large-scale settlement that have been deliberately closed to oriental immigration. Some of them claim that a greater freedom of migration and settlement in the past would have helped to develop more fully the natural resources of the world and, by benefiting all mankind, would have eliminated a major cause of international friction and war.

It has not been possible, unfortunately, to include in the present study a forecast of population growth for the various countries included. Statistical material for even the roughest estimates of trends either does not exist at all or is too unreliable to serve as a basis for such calculations. The subject is complicated, moreover, by the problematic nature of the economic future of various parts of the region and the possibility of rather thorough-going, not to say revolutionary, changes in their cultural adaptations to economic change—more especially, that is, to industrialization and urbanization or, reversely, to a revival of self-supporting native agriculture, involving native customs and family attitudes, in the wake of a diminishing foreign trade. In so far as growth of population is a determining factor in the rise of migration movements, it cannot of course be neglected even in a cursory forecast; and to that extent it is discussed in general descriptive terms.

Nor can this study be enlarged to survey with any thoroughness the population-carrying possibilities of territories potentially in question for resettlement, or to review in any detail—as a possible guide to the future—the experiences of oriental population groups in those non-Asiatic countries which at one time have been open to oriental immigration.[1] However, to complete the general setting of our discussion some of the reasons

[1] A partial survey of this sort—including, outside of Asia, Canada, Australia, the Pacific dependencies of Great Britain, New Zealand, the Soviet Union, and the United States—is made by Norman MacKenzie in *The Legal Status of Aliens in Pacific Countries,* Institute of Pacific Relations, Toronto and New York, 1937.

must briefly be indicated which lead the author to believe that a large inter-migration for permanent settlement between the countries of eastern Asia and the rest of the world lies outside the range of probability in the near future. The two main reasons may be stated categorically without danger of informed contradiction. First, for purposes of oriental settlement the countries with a large white population are not available, simply because that population is opposed to it and has the power to enforce its opposition. Second, whatever population pressures may persist or develop in eastern Asia after the war under the impact of adverse economic conditions, they are not likely to produce a strong desire for settlement in distant parts.

The movement of population from crowded Asiatic countries to other parts of the world has lost one of its main motivating forces. It was set going originally by population pressure but received its modern dimensions from the labor needs of countries in a particular phase of their economic development. Occidental economic expansion to tropical and semi-tropical regions had required, first, the employment of native labor and, when this no longer sufficed, imported slave labor. In course of time, world opinion revolted against the latter, and for it was substituted oriental contract labor. With its aid it was possible to develop the great areas brought under Western control by conquest. But the period of colonial expansion gradually gave way to a period of rational exploitation. Improvements in methods of production and a larger capitalization of large-scale enterprises in proportion to man power have affected the labor requirements. Colonial enterprise no longer is satisfied with docile but ignorant and irresponsible masses of half-starved laborers, physically inefficient and unstable. Processes and tools are tending to become more complicated and necessitate more and more the services of positively interested workers, a low labor turnover.

This technical change affects not only international migratory movements in the East, but also, and more especially, the movement of Asiatic labor to other parts of the world. Quantitative labor requirements come to be more and more modified by qualitative requirements. In many large enterprises today the members of some particular nationality or ethnic group are preferred, not because of some physical advantage which they may possess but because they already have acquired skills, habits, and attitudes that are appreciated by the employers.

Labor recruiting, then, in so far as it is a positive factor in the determination of the volume and direction of international migration, may be expected to become more refined in purposes and methods. However, the strength of migratory movements will be influenced more than in the past by the desires of the potential migratory workers themselves and by the policies of their governments. Recent prewar experience has shown two things: first, that governments are no longer willing to lose the flower of their manhood to some other country if it could be set to increase the economic prosperity of the home country; second, that where labor contracts are made for given periods, whether a season or a term of years, the home governments are more concerned than they were in the past that their subjects shall not be exploited, shall be returned in a better and not in a worse condition than they went. Furthermore, there is a new sense of dignity which expresses itself in strong—sometimes perhaps even excessive—protective measures taken to prevent a labor traffic which would tend to lower the prestige of the nation.[2]

It is probable, as we have seen, that in eastern Asia population pressure as an elementary propulsive force will not be very great immediately after the war, as far as the major reservoirs of labor are concerned. Nevertheless, the desire of men to improve their economic status is universal. Differences in economic opportunity between countries and parts of the world will con-

[2] The Recruiting of Indigenous Workers Convention, 1936, and the Contracts of Employment (Indigenous Workers) Convention, 1939, though far reaching as protective measures in those dependent territories where they have been applied, were further strengthened by a set of recommendations made at the twenty-sixth session of the International Labor Conference, 1944, with the aim of substituting as far as possible a voluntary offer of labor for recruiting, and of legislating the recruiting of workers by private employers out of existence. Steps were recommended, further, "to guard against an undesirable attraction of casual labor to centers of potential employment" and to surround the migrant worker with further safeguards against exploitation and maltreatment. With the provisional agreement shown by all the participant governments, there is reason to believe that these recommendations will soon after the war be embodied in formal international conventions.

tinue to remain very great. Even with a lessened population pressure in the historic areas of high density one would have to expect a continuous flow to the countries with higher labor and living standards of at least the more progressive and adventurous elements—unless artificial barriers were to prevent this equalizing movement of people. In short, the fact that an unusual pressure upon the potential receiving countries in the near future can be avoided, should not be construed as implying that no safeguards need be taken to prevent the influx of immigrants. These safeguards will be as much needed as ever to prevent a deterioration of labor and living standards through the competition of Asiatics accustomed to much lower standards. Free international migration, like free trade, offers no acceptable solution to the complex problems that must be faced. Rather will there be need for new means to raise opportunities of gainful labor everywhere without imperiling the economic status of the more advanced population groups.

Policies of Oriental Exclusion

THERE HAS BEEN much discussion recently in the United States of the merits of various proposals for repealing those sections of the immigration and naturalization laws which discriminate against Orientals and against nationals from a certain zone of southern Asia. Both among the proponents and among the opponents of such measures, this discussion has shown some confusion as regards the nature of the problem. It has swung back and forth from qualitative to quantitative considerations. In some circles the idea persists that additions of oriental stock are especially pernicious to the biological and cultural complex of American society. Others claim that they are free from "race prejudice" but would look with consternation upon any steps that might make it easier for persons from countries with lower living standards to enter the United States. Sometimes even a slight change in the existing restrictions—such as the substitution for complete exclusion of an annual quota of less than a hundred persons—is feared as an "entering wedge" for the resumption of a much larger oriental immigration. Yet others, while they supported the bill enacted in 1943 that recognized

China's desire for a status of racial equality in the American immigration law, fail to recognize that it will be politically unwise to withhold such recognition from other peoples with whom the United States is on a footing of friendly relations. Even as a gesture that act is incomplete, of course, since it still leaves inadmissible to the United States nationals from other countries than China if they happen to be of Chinese "race." And although the special privileges enjoyed by Americans in China under the unequal treaties have been abrogated, only a minority of Americans are ready to concede that, for the sake of a maximum of international collaboration after the war, it is necessary to subject all major policies of international migration to international negotiation instead of regarding them as "strictly domestic" concerns. Not only the potential sending and receiving countries have a stake in the scientific planning and regulation of population exchanges. Considerations of peace and economic stability are involved that concern all peoples.

In the meantime, others of America's Asiatic allies have not failed to take note of the concession made to China's national pride and ere long will demand like treatment. Thus, when Congress adjourned in the summer of 1944, there was before it a bill which would make nationals of India resident in the United States eligible to citizenship. This corresponds to a resolution passed by the Indian Council of State urging the Secretary for External Affairs to obtain that right through diplomatic negotiation. Although one of the smallest of nationality groups in the United States, the Indian minority is the most outspoken of those discriminated against under the immigration law. They now ask that their nationals be permitted to enter the country under the same conditions as the Chinese, and in this demand are backed by some members of Congress and by such influential newspapers as the *New York Times* (February 10, 1944), the *Baltimore Sun* (February 22, 1944), the *Kansas City Star* (March 11, 1944), the *Los Angeles Times* (March 21, 1944), and the *Columbia, S. C., Record* (April 7, 1944). Virtual exclusion of the Filipinos from continental United States rests on an agreement; but the stigma of undesirability has been removed by a token admission of Filipinos to the United States and by conceding to those resident there the right to become naturalized in certain circumstances. Burma, after the achievement of independence, and Thailand hardly can be expected to stay behind; and the colonial governments of Malaya, Indo-China, and the Netherlands Indies, however little disposed to favor increased direct contacts of their subjects with the United States, may soon be forced by their rising national sentiment to make similar claims in their behalf.

Issues that involve national susceptibilities are sometimes best resolved by tackling first those humanitarian aspects about which practical agreements can be reached. These in turn will affect the character of the more difficult negotiations. For this reason if for no other, importance attaches to some of the recommendations made by the International Labor Conference at its Philadelphia session in 1944 on the subject of international migration. (See above, p. 156.) Although these relate to the movement of workers to and from dependent territories, at least the same protections as those recommended will be demanded by world opinion for workers invited to fill a labor shortage in the more advanced independent countries. Already the war-time arrangements made for the reception of Mexican and West Indian agricultural laborers in the United States, insuring terms of employment for the immigrant worker no less favorable than those customary in the localities where they are employed, and insuring the safe return of the workers at the end of the contract period with their savings intact, represent a great social advance over the conditions which oriental labor immigrants had to face in the past.[3]

Oriental exclusion from the Americas, from Australia, and from Africa—not to complicate the picture with reference to regions manifestly unsuitable to receive large alien additions to their population—involves three separate problems. There are, first of all, actually under-populated areas which, whether by national planning or under some concerted international plan, may either be reserved for the growth of the native population or be opened to immigrants. Second, there are areas which it is in the world interest to bar altogether against the influx of population from outside. Such areas may include reservations for ethnic groups as

[3] See, for example, B. Lasker, *Filipino Immigration*, Chicago, 1931, Chapter VIII.

yet little advanced in civilization that need a relatively large
amount of land for their primitive mode of living. They may
include geologically new lands on which agriculturally utile
soil is only in process of formation—lands which in their present
state may easily be denuded by the activities of pioneer settlers.
They may include lands covered with valuable growths, such as
forests, the destruction of which would more than offset the
economic gains from clearing and cultivation of the soil. They
also include lands so poor that they would not repay the capital
investment necessary for their cultivation or would condemn
those who might settle them to a life of abject poverty. At a
time when large population groups have been dislocated by war
there is special danger that any halfway promising refuge may
be opened to them and that they themselves may eagerly em-
brace the offered opportunity to start a new life far from the sites
of bitter memories. The question should always be asked whether
they are likely to stay or whether, with a return of self-con-
fidence and with the aid of small savings, they will soon take
advantage of better opportunities that may offer elsewhere or
even, after an interval of years, wish to return to their former
homeland. When that happens, valuable investments may be
lost; the sense of failure experienced by those governments and
private organizations that have sponsored the settlement project
may predispose them against other projects of more lasting value.
A similar misadventure to be avoided is a settlement of immigrants insufficiently controlled to guarantee the continuation of
the economy for which it is planned. The animosities against
alien settlements in different parts of the world often derive
from the discrepancy between the forms of production for which
members of a given ethnic group were originally introduced and
the economic functions which they afterward assumed—sometimes including the exhaustion of natural resources, or domination of the native economy, or simply failure to stay on the land.

The third major category of problems consists of questions
that relate to the social and political by-products of population
policy, and in connection with our study more especially to the
forms and consequences of oriental exclusion.

To begin with the first group of problems, those connected
with differential material possibilities of large-scale settlement,

one must, of course, take account of the geographical location and the nature of the seemingly under-populated territories, and of the type of development of which each of them is capable. Magnificent schemes based on nothing more than land measurements and population statistics are not only futile but also dangerous; for, they are liable to arouse, among the ignorant, hopes far from possibilities of realization. Prospects of ability to support a larger population are always relative to the cost of planting it and to the value of whatever wealth that population under the given circumstances—its state of civilization, the capital available, prospects of markets, and others—might be expected to be able to produce. Even in a densely populated area, in our most crowded cities, there is always room for those whose exceptional ability or combination of qualities can create social values out of the specific materials to be found there. And probably only an occasional solitude-loving philosopher or landscape painter could hope to create wealth in the bleak expanse of a waterless desert. Indeed, recent experience in many parts of the world tends to indicate that, generally speaking, the possible intensification of land uses, and hence the ability to support population, of naturally rich areas has in the past been underassessed, and the population-carrying capacity of naturally poor areas has been exaggerated—at least in popular opinion. The distribution of mineral wealth below the surface complicates the situation but does not greatly alter it.

The Case of Australia

THERE IS A LARGE LITERATURE concerning the peopling of the world's remaining "wide open spaces." Orientals complain of being cheated of their share in humanity's common birthright when Western powers reserve large land areas for a sprinkling of white population or try to keep out all newcomers; and this complaint has a semblance of justification when such areas are nearer to Asia than they are to Europe. When they read speeches made by public officials and resolutions passed even by trade-union organizations calling for millions of European immigrants to help in the more rapid peopling of Australia, for example, they wonder whether the countries dominated by the West alone

161

stand in need of defensive preparation against future aggression. They also wonder whether a fraction of the money that would be needed to bring water to the parched plains of western Australia or to make the highlands of New Guinea habitable if employed to develop the resources of eastern Asia would not contribute far more to the wealth and the security of the world. For, only a few years ago, it had been understood among informed people that the "wide open spaces," now suddenly regarded as suitable for white colonization, were a mirage and not a promise. A well-known Australian historian, the late Sir Ernest Scott, used to say he wished map-makers would color the bulk of Australia as blue as the surrounding seas so as to get rid of the erroneous notion that it could be made habitable for large numbers. Indeed, recent scientific studies show that, except for a few small spots in the South and West, the more or less densely populated eastern coast belt of that continent is the only part of it which, without an unremunerative capital investment, could stand a somewhat larger population. Even the inner margins of that belt, which at one time seemed to hold out hope for a further development of dry-farming, have proved disappointing; and especially the small cultivator with little capital would be quite lost there.[4]

With the adoption of the Atlantic Charter by the United Nations, both European and Asiatic population problems have entered a new era of international consideration. There is every prospect that in the concerted planning for economic reconstruction these problems will not be permitted to be made the football of mutually exclusive national policies but will be considered in their relation to other matters that can be settled only through a stressing of common needs. Recent influential statements in Australia [5] give a forecast of this saner and more realistic atti-

[4] W. D. Forsyth, in *The Myth of Open Spaces* (Melbourne and New York, 1942) discusses also the more difficult question of Australia's industrial possibilities as a means of supporting a larger population—without arriving at very encouraging results.

[5] In addition to W. D. Forsyth, *op. cit.*, see also the same author's "Stability in the Pacific: The Position of Australia" and "White Australia and the Charter," by a Member of the Sydney Branch, Australian Institute of International Affairs, both in *Australia and the Pacific*, New York, 1942, mim., I, 19-27 and 82-90.

tude. That the Australian policy of oriental exclusion was in part dictated by fear and prejudice is admitted. But more important is the admission that nations which for adequate reasons cannot open their doors to oriental immigration have nevertheless the duty—if only in the interest of preserving peace—of contributing in other ways to the relief of Asiatic population pressures. Even the contention that emigration affords only temporary relief is no excuse for the politically and economically stronger nations to let the feeling of frustration which their negative attitude has produced among Orientals continue to produce international friction.

Australia [writes the Sydney author] should explicitly abandon the term "White Australia," explain its immigration policy in terms of its economic and social ends, demonstrate that "keeping other people out" is by no means the sum and substance of our national policy. We believe, we have a right to control the composition of our population, but we also acknowledge the duty and responsibility to act as a "good neighbor" in a world order. Neighbors co-operate, and we should link with our "negative" immigration policy a "positive" policy of full participation in world trade.[6]

What is needed [writes W. D. Forsyth] is not open spaces but open doors. . . . The right to live implies an obligation to let live, and the White Australia Policy could not be justified if it denied the means of existence to the Japanese, Chinese, and other peoples.[7]

How much weight is to be attached to pronouncements of this sort and what contributions they will actually make to the peaceful co-operation of Occidentals and Orientals it would be difficult to say. Recent news from Australia leaves no doubt that the intention is to open the doors of the continent to immigration; but thus far no one in authority has given the green light to Orientals.[8] Percy J. Clarey, President of the Australasian Council of Trade Unions, and delegate to the International Labor Conference at Philadelphia in May, 1944, gave it as his view that "under proper development and safeguards against deterioration

[6] *Op. cit.*, p. 89, note 60.

[7] *Australia and the Pacific*, p. 27.

[8] *E.g., Christian Science Monitor*, January 1, July 2, July 7, November 2, 1943, February 4, April 24, June 2, 1944.

of social and economic standards, Australia could support a population of from 150 to 200 million people." Other Australians, especially those who have made technical studies of the problem, would consider even an increase of population from 7 to 30 million very difficult to accomplish but are agreed that if it were necessary for the defense of the Dominion, the country could support a substantially increased population.[9] There is, however, always the demand that this increase derive as much as possible from a rise in the Australian birth-rate and that, in as far as it must in part come from immigration, this must be white and preferably British immigration.

Recently the recognition that a liberalization of the Dominion's immigration policy is inevitable, has led to a growing sympathy with a plan to open up certain regions, such as Kimberley in northwestern Australia, to settlement by Jewish refugees. This plan has been approved by organized labor as well as by those civic and liberal groups, churches, and employer associations which would naturally tend to support such a movement on humanitarian or business grounds. Evidently the organizers believe that because of its special character as part of a world effort to rehabilitate an ethnic group that has suffered greatly from the brutality of the Axis, this plan can be financed even if its economic soundness cannot be foreseen with any certainty. Others doubt the wisdom of yet another colonization scheme that may lead to failure and undermine Australia's reputation as a promising place of settlement for the sort of people the Commonwealth really wants but can get only in small volume at best, namely western European, especially British, agriculturists and skilled industrial workers. By the severe tests which Jewish organizations have in the past applied to proposed settlement schemes in Latin America and elsewhere, the Kimberley project is only moderately attractive. The climate, though tolerable, is unpropitious for a self-sufficient agricultural economy by a colony of Europeans. The soil and water conditions are excellent, but not for large continuous areas. The region is most suitable for a pastural economy—but this with the usual diffi-

[9] The war-time motivation of the changing trend in Australia's population policy is discussed by Howard Daniel and Minnie Bell in "Manpower in Australia," *Far Eastern Survey*, XIII, 3 (February 9, 1944), 24-8.

culties in a tropical region. Because of the isolation of the settlement from markets, the trade commodities would have to be large to pay for the necessarily heavy cost of development (such as irrigation) and of transportation. There would be no source of cheap colored labor to assist either in that development or in agricultural production.[10] There would be opportunities for associating industries with the production of raw materials but except for the production of articles for local consumption, the manufactures—meat packing, for example—would necessarily have to compete with those of more favorably situated regions.[11] The Jewish community of Australia, about 30,000, though prosperous, is far too small to support an experiment which is proposed to absorb eventually some fifty thousand Jewish refugees; the financial risks would have to be carried elsewhere.

As long as it were purely philanthropic in character, such a colonization project for European refugees would probably not be resented by oriental nationals even though they themselves were to remain virtually excluded from Australia. Some increase in the European population of a continent as large as Europe may have to be assured before it is safe to invite Orientals with much lower living standards to enter the Commonwealth in any large number; but it is difficult to envisage a peaceful future for Australia if it continues to flout the national and racial pride of Asiatics.

Only exceptionally favorable political conditions have permitted them the luxury of such an attitude. They could never have retained their enormous territories without the protection assured them by the British navy—which by the way has not restrained them these last few years from a persistent refusal to receive among them British unemployed.[12]

[10] The sparsity of indigenous population is, however, also an advantage since it relieves the promoters of the need for tedious and often difficult dispossession proceedings.

[11] I. N. Steinberg, *A Jewish Settlement in Australia,* Freeland League, New York, 1944, pamphlet; Shirley Jenkins, "Refugee Settlement in Australia," *Far Eastern Survey,* XIII, 13 (June 28, 1944), 120-2, for a description of the area: A. C. Angelo, "Colonization of the East Kimberleys," *Walkabout,* April 1, 1941, p. 13, map, il.

[12] Gaston Bouthoul, *La Population dans le Monde,* Paris, 1935, p. 175.

Australian policy in this matter may, indeed, prove of critical importance to the security of the Pacific and to world peace. Abandonment of the "White Australia" policy obviously would afford no lasting relief for population pressure in any of the countries to the north. The few million Javanese, Chinese, or Japanese who might be admitted to the continent would soon be replaced in their homeland by a larger survival. But it is now admitted by informed Australians that the Commonwealth cannot wait to have its optimum of perhaps twice its present population of not quite 7.5 million made up by a higher birth rate [13] and a practically nonexistent British farmer emigration. Therefore an annual immigration of 30,000 or 50,000 persons would be in line with a prudent policy of economic development.[14] The question then is whether it is safe either for Australia or for the British Commonwealth and its associates to permit this immigration to be tinged with an outmoded race prejudice which, in a period of many international and interracial tensions, might easily become a cause of acute controversy.

Some Other Potential Receiving Countries

NEW ZEALAND also experienced a serious shortage in manpower when war came.[15] Although this country, with a population of 1,641,000 in 1940, cannot possibly contribute much to its military security through an increase in population, nevertheless a great effort in that direction is widely demanded. Professor H. Belshaw, the well-known Auckland University economist, in a recent article has deflated some of the wilder proposals and pointed to the great difficulty of carrying out even so modest a plan as the admission of 70,000 immigrants per annum over a period of years.[16] He believes that an absorption capacity of

[13] After a steady decline for many decades, Australia's net rate of reproduction has increased a little in recent years; but the demographic composition of the population is such that population experts do not expect this upward trend to continue for long.

[14] Lewis L. Lorwin, *Postwar Plans of the United Nations*, New York, 1943, pp. 209-10; Karl J. Pelzer, *Population and Land Utilization in the Pacific Area*, New York, 1941, pp. 60-1.

[15] *Pacific Affairs*, XVII, 1 (March, 1944), 42.

[16] "Population and Immigration," New Zealand *Financial Times*, February, 1944.

20,000 per year would be nearer the mark, with the aim of reaching a population of two and a half million in fifty years.

Other circles in New Zealand are less conservative. A Dominion Settlement Association has been formed to advance the country's security through a larger population. But the very purpose made implicit the demand that immigration should be white and preferably British. Indeed, to judge from some of the concrete plans proposed, the supporters of the movement think almost exclusively of British immigration.[17] It may be expected, perhaps, that after the panic is over which Japan's southward advance produced in the Dominions during the early stages of the war, the old dislike for population increase through immigration will re-assert itself. If not, the difficulty of maintaining friendly and co-operative relations with China and India on the basis of racial discrimination could only be avoided by making the liberalization of admission requirements a matter of internal empire policy and a matter of emergency relief for European Jews, to the exclusion of Danes and other "desirable" Europeans as well as of Orientals.

Limitations of space do not permit the author to pursue this subject by exploring possibilities of admission for Orientals in Africa and Latin America. On the former continent Indians were in recent times the only Asiatics with a distinct economic function which they could have any hope of expanding under favorable circumstances. These circumstances, however, have been receding much on the same grounds as in Burma: Indians have gone to East and South Africa to extract wealth, not to create it. Their presence has been increasingly resented, and no one familiar with the situation seems to favor Indian settlements.[18] The history of Chinese in Africa has been similar to that in Australia and in North America. They were welcome in the

[17] A plan to bring in a million war orphans in the course of ten years; a plan to attract thousands of British officers stationed in India; a plan to admit British soldiers of the laboring class, now in Africa. Prime Minister Peter Fraser at the time of the Canberra Conference, spring of 1944, made no bones about New Zealand not wanting "an influx of people with low economic levels." (See *Christian Science Monitor*, March 8, 1944, p. 9.)

[18] See Julian Huxley, *Africa View*, New York, 1931, p. 438; Sarah Gertrude Millin, *The South Africans*, New York, 1927, Chapter VI—to mention two outstanding liberals and internationalists.

early days of mining developments, and some of them grew rich through trade and speculation; but the conditions for a large and permanent agricultural colonization by Chinese did not exist. The Japanese have not even attempted such colonization.

Chinese experience in Latin America has not been very different from that in North America. Peru and other countries attempted to recruit Chinese immigrants when all attempts to attract European immigrants had failed. Those who came soon engaged in trade, often in severe competition with the native retailers. Only a few years ago riots occurred in Mexico through such rivalry, and restrictions have been adopted by most of the republics to keep Chinese immigrants out. The planting of Japanese agricultural colonies has been a different story. Although economic in purpose, it had all the earmarks of imperialist expansion and strategic placement for securing particular raw materials in case of war.[19] Brazil and Peru, which before the war had the largest number of Japanese residents (in 1938, Brazil 170,000 and Peru 22,000), are not likely to open their doors widely to Orientals when the chances of receiving desirable immigrants from Europe after the war are going to be so much brighter than at any time in the recent past.

It is possible, of course, that an entirely different atmosphere will prevail in the world after the war, and that the representatives of nations sitting around the council table to make plans for a better distribution of world population will consider only the population-carrying capacity of diverse territories and the needs and talents of peoples suffering from lack of living space. But at the time of writing, Utopia still seems a long way off. The best that can be hoped for, apparently, is a series of bilateral agreements through which countries desirous of developing their natural resources more rapidly will try to assure themselves of an influx of those nationals who at the time seem most suitable and most responsive to their call.

[19] J. F. Normano and Antonello Gerbi, *The Japanese in South America*, New York, 1943.

16

TEMPORARY MEASURES OF RELIEF

Trade Opportunity

IN THE PAST, too many Western students of Eastern population problems have pointed to industrialization and birth control as the means by which the necessity for emigration on the part of oriental peoples could be avoided. But their studies did not often extend to those occidental pressures upon these peoples, which narrowed down the practicability of seemingly obvious economic and political solutions. The pre-war era was one not only of increasing obstruction against international, and especially oriental, migration; it was also an era of increasing obstruction against the freedom of world trade. In times of widespread depression and of famine, simple peasant peoples cling only the more tenaciously to their tradition of large families; and conditions are certainly not favorable to a large advance in industrial enterprise. The colonial character of trade relations in a large part of the Pacific—and of the world—obscured the opportunities for mutually advantageous exchanges of commodities between the peoples of the industrially less advanced countries, besides blocking the access of colonial producers to the most advantageous outside markets. In these respects, and others, the term "semi-colonial" has been applicable to such countries as China and Siam—now Thailand—countries which have never been in a position to develop either their potential producing capacity or their potential foreign trade. And the frantic effort of Japan to escape the same fate has been a contributory cause of the growth of aggressive militarism in that country.

Frank W. Notestein, in an aside to his recent study of population prospects in Europe, says that the problems of demographic development of large areas in eastern Asia are of longer range and ultimately more serious than those of Europe, but involve the same underlying principles:

Broadly speaking, the nations of the West have two choices: that of sitting on the lid as long as possible, in the substantial certainty of being blown off eventually to face well-earned animosities; or that of fostering a social, economic, and political development of these areas which will release some of the pressure of population on developed resources and ultimately check the rapid growth of peoples.[1]

It is not possible within the limits of the present study to explore the ways in which the adoption of a new commercial policy on the part of the more powerful countries—a policy returning to the use of high tariff rates only for the protection of infant industries and other special purposes—may help to reduce population pressures. But it may be said in passing that a liberalized trade policy is not the only means by which such countries as the United States and the British Dominions can effect that purpose without relinquishing their refusal to admit oriental immigrants other than in token numbers. Especially the former can do much through its influence on the flow of capital in post war years. Indirect discriminations in the allocation of shipping can be removed. Marketing facilities and facilities for transshipment can be improved.

Short-Term Labor Migration

ONE MAY EVEN SAY that a wider cognizance of the different causes of population pressure and a more widespread understanding of the different kinds of migration and their different effects on the receiving countries would help. Popular attitudes toward immigration in general or toward immigration from particular countries and regions have been colored by an undiscriminating antagonism to possible encroachments upon the accustomed way of life, and sometimes by racial pride and prejudice. Back of these attitudes lies the assumption that immigration necessarily means a permanent addition to the population and a sharpened competition for land and jobs. But this is by no means always the case—and need not be the case at all

[1] "Some Implications of Population Change for Post-war Europe," *Proceedings of the American Philosophical Society*, LXXXVII, 2 (1943), 174.

if all immigration were made for a limited duration only (except for strictly defined special classes of persons) and regulated by actual needs, impartially ascertained.

Restrictive immigration policies under modern conditions sometimes overshoot their mark when, in addition to keeping out undesired newcomers and preventing the growth of population through external accretions, they also keep out those who come to render, for a limited time and under controlled conditions, services that are highly beneficial to the whole community. The possibilities of fast and cheap migration have been increased by modern air transportation. It is as easy today—or will be soon—for an artisan to extend his search for work to a continent as but recently it was to extend it to the surrounding counties. Shall this great advantage to the mobility of labor and the flexibility of enterprise—seasonably and cyclically—be sacrificed on the altar of patriotic misconceptions, or can it be utilized to raise standards of living and to ease international relations?

One should not forget, either, the broadening effect of travel and foreign residence as important elements in the adjustment of tradition-bound nations and classes to new conditions. The enormous economic and social changes now under way in China, for example, are unthinkable except for the influence of large numbers who have experienced contacts with a different social world. And this influence is greatest where the emigrants have been permitted to mingle freely with men of other races and cultures. But even without such mingling, the very fact of a temporary escape from the binding rules of the home society or the forced association abroad between members of classes that have little in common at home may help to break down some of the walls that stand in the way of progress. Often it is only through new adaptations between people and resources that the population-supporting capacity of a given area can be raised. Thus, for example, John Wesley Coulter, in a recent study of Fiji, points out that the very necessity of association produced by contract labor abroad for Indian emigrants have for the time being—and probably with lasting effects—eliminated those caste distinctions and segregations which are among the greatest causes of frustration, inefficiency, and poverty in India.[2]

[2] *Fiji, Little India of the Pacific,* Chicago, 1942, p. 101.

171

It is true, if every labor scarcity, from whatever cause, could immediately be ended with the introduction of a sufficient number of temporary migrants to meet the need, native labor would be unable to bargain for a larger share in the product of agriculture or industry. And this would be true even if employers could be forced to grant no worse conditions of employment to immigrant than to native labor. Nevertheless, no one will contend that the working population of California has suffered from the directed and regulated influx of migrant farm workers in recent years. It is conceivable that, in the common interest and with the co-operation of organized labor in detailed decisions, the international flow of labor also could be made freer—through international agreements under which a temporary influx of workers could be used to keep down the cost of living rather than the cost of labor. Such a situation happens to exist in the United States today. While millions of American farmers and farm laborers are under arms, a fairly large Mexican, West Indian, or oriental labor contingent could be absorbed in agricultural occupations with obvious benefit to the whole country, and indeed to the whole world—provided these temporary visitors received the standard wage and could with ease be sent home as soon as Americans were available to resume the jobs held by aliens.

However, the fulfillment of these conditions cannot, in the light of our national history of labor relations, be assumed. Even if they were embodied in international agreements, they might not always be interpreted impartially. There is good reason for the popular fear of *any* large-scale immigration even if only temporary and surrounded by all possible safeguards against its use to keep down the price of labor. Only a very different distribution of power between employing and employed groups would take the social risk out of such an arrangement.

Moreover, this discussion cannot be said to be complete if it leaves entirely out of account the non-economic aspects of the problem. For example, the antagonism to Japanese immigration in the United States, and also in Mexico and Peru, was largely motivated by a feeling, since proved sound enough, that it was promoted for political and strategic purposes quite as much as economic ones. While the hospitality of a country cannot be greatly misused by temporary visitors without right of permanent domicile, nevertheless a fear of sinister motives might survive. More important is the feeling, prevalent in all countries of white settlement, that the cultural homogeneity of society is threatened through the influx of groups with a totally different and presumably inassimilable cultural tradition. In theory this would not affect attitudes toward even fairly large groups of *temporary* immigrants; but in actuality it has shown itself strong enough, in their case too, to prevent amicable social relations. In short, however deplorable they may seem from the moral standpoint, unfavorable inter-ethnic attitudes are a reality, too, that cannot rapidly be expunged.

International Amenity

WITH THE RECOGNITION, then, that few areas under occidental control offer even restricted opportunities for the hard-pressed and land-poor Oriental, we return to the third of the problem areas indicated above: that relating to the forms and methods of regulation, restriction, and exclusion. This problem affects our study only indirectly, since it does not deal with actual possibilities of resettlement but only with the resentments aroused by the political measures which close them. We need therefore deal with it only in passing.

The history of American-Japanese relations has, of course, largely hinged on the mutual recriminations incident to the exclusion of Japanese immigrants. As had already been noted, the turn which Japanese foreign policy took in this century was influenced by the experience of similar rebuffs to those of our immigration law of 1924 in many parts of the world. Our Chinese exclusion law, already referred to, dates back to 1882 and, likewise, never ceased to rankle in the minds of Chinese patriots until it was rescinded. No responsible Asiatics have in recent times demanded unconditional access for their nationals to the territories under occidental sovereignty. What they are asking for—and not least emphatically among them the Indians— is that they should not be discriminated against as members of inferior races, but that the conditions of their admission or exclusion be the same as those operating in the case of Europeans.

This dispute does not, of course, affect only the United States but also the British Dominions, several if not all of the Latin American Republics, and many other states. Under the cleansing fire of the World War, the United Nations have pledged themselves to aims of postwar reconstruction which preclude the perpetuation of those undeniable injuries—at least to self-respect if not to more material interests—which discriminatory immigration laws have inflicted upon the peoples of certain races. However, traditional prejudices still are so strong in several of these countries, our own included, that effective campaigns of popular education are needed to eliminate even those discriminations which contribute nothing to national protection against unwanted immigration. The Axis governments have been able, in their propaganda among colored peoples, to utilize the existing evidence that, despite their democratic theories, most of the United Nations in the West discriminate against the greater part of the world's population because of their skin color.

A decent mutual respect between peoples and races is the first requisite for any policy that may be designed to prevent differential rates of population growth from becoming even more serious sources of international friction in the future. Such a policy must take into account many other factors besides the uneven distribution of population in relation to resources. As long as cultures and civilizations differ as greatly as they now do, there can be no equilibrium. The different attitudes toward size of families may perhaps eventually disappear under the impact of more similar economic experiences. However, these attitudes may also be artificially influenced by national policy, as they were only so recently in Germany, Italy, and Japan. The economic and cultural relations between nations may again, after this war, determine whether some people or other will, in order to protect and enhance its own political prospects, stimulate an abnormal population growth, whether some people or other will lose its will to live and decline in numbers. All questions of population growth and exchange are, therefore, connected with even larger questions of world policy.

174

PART VI

CONCLUSIONS

GENERAL CONCLUSIONS

In the course of the preceding discussion, a number of general conclusions have been intimated. In part they were generalizations from historical experience in eastern Asia, and in part indications of trends leading over into the postwar era. We found that international migration in that region has in the main been of three kinds: the formation of colonies in the wake of international trade; the overflow into foreign territory of migration movements that are essentially internal; induced migration to further specific economic or political interests.

The formation of small enclaves of aliens in connection with foreign trade is very old in Asia. Through natural increase and through accretion, such colonies have become the nuclei of much larger alien communities, and through intermarriage and assimilation they have facilitated the further immigration and absorption of members of the same or kindred ethnic groups.

Overflows of internal population movements into foreign territory have peopled most of the countries of Southeast Asia and have added to their population through the centuries. They have also peopled the coastal region of Northeast Asia and spilled over into Mongolia. They have been both the cause and the consequence of wars of invasion. The recent westward flow of Chinese population is only an example of many events in which military pressure applied at one point has led to expansion at another.

Since the middle of the nineteenth century, the regimentation

175

of contract labor in connection with large-scale agricultural and industrial enterprise, mostly in foreign ownership and under foreign control, has been the largest single cause of international migration in eastern Asia. We have avoided use of the word "coolie" because of its unfavorable connotations; but we may as well recognize the truth that the most important projects of economic development in modern times, involving the largest shifts of population, have not been achieved with the labor of free men. There have in recent decades been notable improvements, through international agreement, in methods of labor recruiting, in the protection of migrants while in transit, and in the conditions of employment; but the migrant workers for the most part were propelled by misery. If the declared war aims of the United Nations should prevail, there would be little left of this type of labor migration. However, even our ablest statesmen can produce no miracles. It will take many generations before the uneven distribution of population in relation to natural resources—so direful for the breadwinner and so advantageous for his exploiter—can be remedied.

RESOURCES AND ADAPTABILITY

THE EFFECT of the uneven growth of population on the future migratory movements in Asia is especially difficult to assess. For this itself is largely a matter of policy, direct and indirect. Some governments will go to great lengths to encourage larger families, others will accept a rising rate of reproduction as an inevitable though not especially desired by-product of economic plans. Thus, Vice-President Wallace, on his return from Siberia and China, on July 9, 1944, reported:

Soviet Asia during the last fifteen years has more than doubled in population. It is quite possible that the next fifty years will see a further increase of more than thirty million people. I am convinced from what I saw of the Amur River region that in the southern part of that area there will be a great increase in population. . . . Most of the people who moved to Siberia with their factories will stay there.

It so happened that on the same day the Supreme Soviet promulgated a law on marriage and family from which it appears that a speeding up of human reproduction must be regarded as one of the central social policies of the Soviet Union. In China, on the other hand, vast plans for social reconstruction have been announced which will intensify production and lower the death-rate, thus incidentally speed up the increase of population; and this consequence is accepted as perhaps unavoidable but certainly not as an end to be desired.

Redistribution of population in the years to come will be influenced more than in the past by technical change and by the unevenness of its occurrence in different parts of the world and even between neighboring countries. Already it has affected important areas of production in the East. It is bound to affect more, and these to an ever-increasing degree. The substitutions of materials in industries of many kinds have gone so far of late that no sensible person will insist today on the immutable need of the world for this metal or that textile fiber. An industrialist recently computed that "some 10,000 men in American factories can produce as much [synthetic rubber] as 300,000 natives on Far Eastern plantations [can produce of the natural sap]." [1] On the other hand, not a month passes but the interested reader discovers some new and important industrial use for an Asiatic or tropical material previously used only for very limited purposes. Take, for example, some of the new uses of tree oils, of rare minerals, of various fibers and barks, of skins, algae, and nuts. Just as the world's demand for rice and soy bean, for cotton and silk, for tin and petroleum, have produced population differentials in the era just past, so new demands—and, no less important, the passing of some old ones—must influence the distribution of population in the new era. There may be altogether too many mouths to feed in India or Tonkin or Java as the machine encroaches upon the traditional sphere of human labor; but there may also be far too few inhabitants in such places as western China, Borneo, the Shan States—too few in relation to their potential resources—to satisfy the purchasing agents and importers of the industrial regions.

And this is only one of many primary economic influences to be anticipated. Even more far-reaching, perhaps, will be that of

[1] Francis Westbrook, Jr., "The Chemical Revolution," *The Nation*, August 7, 1943, p. 153.

a vastly improved system of communication. For, time, distance, and cost of transportation rather than a fortuitous political pattern have held up the currents of trade and, with them, the streams of human migration. Poles laid across roads, passports and visas, troublesome inspections at the docks—such things do not in themselves constitute serious barriers to international migration, in Asia or elsewhere. Restrictions and prohibitions in the national interest will continue, may even for some time be sharper than ever before. But there is also a mutual interest between nations in a larger flow of migration. It is difficult to envisage in all its importance the role which safe and easy internal communications will play in the readjustment of population to resources, especially in those parts of eastern Asia where internal economic development has been sacrificed to the demands of foreign trade. In this connection, we have found that in almost all parts of that region there are possibilities of settling population groups without sending them abroad, by opening up areas that are economically marginal only in terms of a narrowly conceived agrarian civilization. In the mountains of Sumatra and Malaya, in the interior of Borneo and Cambodia, in Inner Mongolia and Sinkiang, even in the assumedly crowded Japanese and Philippine Islands, almost everywhere opportunities of remunerative modern mixed farming, of combination of farming with animal husbandry, or of both with small-scale industry, await capital and man power.

Those are the two crucial factors. Capital is not something that flows from granite bank buildings in London and Amsterdam and New York, or from national treasuries. The banks and the treasury departments are not sources but regulators. The present war is destroying capital on an unprecedented scale. Only creative work can reproduce it. The larger plans of industrialization, of railway building, and so forth, attractive and practical though many of them are, will in many instances have to wait. But we have looked at examples—one could not do more —showing that even relatively small investments of capital can in industrially retarded countries often create conditions that make for an appreciably higher output and a corresponding absorption of surplus labor.

As for the human element, ability has neither racial nor geo-

178

graphical limits. Roughly 600 million people inhabit the region we have been considering, and some 150 million of these inhabit the tropical zone. That does not mean they are constitutionally incapable of doing a good day's work. It does mean that they can achieve their maximum productivity only under conditions that allow for the climate and for the mode of life which has become habitual in effective adjustment to the climate. Much of the labor migration in Asia and elsewhere was injurious to all interests but those of the promoters. It was condoned because of a widespread fundamental error: the assumption that if you want to achieve a maximum of economic activity in the tropics you must transplant workers there from the Temperate Zone. In practice, this policy has only meant that the natives often have had no share in the advantages of modern enterprise and that the energy and the health of the first generation of immigrant workers has been exploited. When they settled and their children became acclimatized there was no longer a noteworthy difference between their physical ability and that of the native people. In other words, if spontaneous internal mobility and managed resettlement take care of overpopulation in such countries as India and China, realistic and humane labor policies can solve problems of seeming under-population in tropical Asia.

Yes, the native is too lazy to work. Why should he work on plantations and in mines under the terms he has been offered in the past?

Another neglected human resource is that of skill. Several of the Asiatic governments have discovered this latent resource but have been slow to bring it into use. As large-scale machine production standardizes and cheapens basic commodities and brings them into ever wider use, the plane of living rises both quantitatively and qualitatively. The beginnings of industrialization in the countries of eastern Asia with their low average purchasing power bring a greater variety of goods within the reach of the consumer. They also have an educational effect that redounds to the advantage of those engaged in the domestic crafts: spending power which formerly was exhausted in purchases of familiar local objects becomes accustomed to a wider choice; and so greater specialization and quantity production becomes possible also for the home industries. The revival and perfection of traditional crafts thus will—perhaps more in Asia than anywhere else—absorb much of the productive energy of the people in the period of economic reconstruction, without having to wait for large investments of capital and heavy industries.

We know little about the shifts of population produced by the war itself where it has been waged against civilians as well as between armies. The magnitude of the refugee problem will probably prove to be much smaller in eastern Asia than in Europe. It may be more difficult for a simple peasant to re-establish himself when he has been ejected from his home than it is for a mechanic or a clerk; but the peasant is always a potential general laborer and as such more easily placed in useful employment than almost any other category of worker. He also is more capable than most other occupational types when it comes to the necessity of keeping alive in a wilderness. So, the task of resettling war refugees in eastern Asia, however large it may appear on paper, will in practice be mainly one of transportation, of equipment with rather simple tools, of tiding them over the period of preparation until the first crops are harvested—altogether a much less costly venture than the settlement of a similar number of workers in the West.

A certain amount of regimentation will be necessary to prevent economic disaster for many thousands of people, East as well as West, when the flood of government purchases subsides and when carefully nurtured little enclaves of economic opportunity are rudely broken into by returned warriors. However, such a regimentation will not, we have been assured by the leaders of the United Nations, be for a return to the *status quo ante*. It will for the disinherited be an orderly march into a brighter future.

Not only on technical grounds but through the inner logic of postwar developments there is the likelihood of a great increase in general mobility. In times of cut-throat competition and of fear of aggression, restrictive immigration laws are drawn up, existing regulations are sharpened and more rigidly enforced. Internal disorder conduces to absentee landlordism and thus to excessive rents and debts that bind the peasant to the soil. A more general security makes it easier for men to take a chance and find a job away from home or buy a farm at a distance.

However, the increased mobility from this particular cause is not of wide range: it evens out inequalities of opportunity within the county or the province. To enlarge its scope and thus make it really effective in decanting surplus population from too densely populated areas, the means and the machinery must be provided. Just to tell an Ilocano sharecropper that he can go to Mindanao or to tell a Chinese laborer that there is a better-paid job waiting for him in the mines of Billiton is not enough. There is need for information services, for planned transportation, for secure financial arrangements so that stay-at-home dependents may be supported. Above all, where an economic project calls for the employment of immigrant labor, conditions must be made fit for that labor. In some instances, areas have been opened for settlement which, on grounds of health, should never have been opened at all, however rich the soil. In other instances, settlement projects have been conceived and carried out on so insufficient a scale that the output was far too small to pay for the cost of development. Again, permanent communities have been established to exploit resources—lumber, for example —all too soon exhausted and leaving the settlers stranded and bankrupt.

Relief and Population Policy

BEFORE ATTEMPTING to summarize the major tasks that spring from the conditions described for joint international action in the field of population policy in eastern Asia, it will be well to consider briefly the immediate emergency tasks of migrant relief and rehabilitation. These tasks are distinct from the larger tasks and cannot wait. Indeed, in some instances the military and naval authorities will have to proceed with operations to facilitate the return and re-establishment of masses of people before the national authorities can adequately function in these respects. But such emergency operations cannot be altogether separated in design or effect from the incipient larger plans. They will inevitably influence the direction of policy and the predisposition of the population groups affected to co-operate with the authorities.

Mention has already been made (p. 24) of some of the special difficulties inherent in oriental society when it comes to the application of effective programs motivated by concerns of social welfare and implemented with modern techniques. While such plans can be superimposed upon older methods rooted in the traditional family and community system, their success depends largely on carrying along public opinion. In so far as the old ways are inadequate for dealing with vast contemporary emergencies, the new ways must be demonstrably superior if they are to be widely accepted.

For those national and international officers who will be charged with the care and transplantation of war-displaced civilian populations it is especially important to know something of the differences between the social situations likely to be encountered in Eastern Asia from those in Europe. The Asiatic refugee has not usually left behind him an elaborate system of public services. Unless he comes from one of the modern cities, he will know little of the intricate economic organization that supplies the Westerner with the diversified ingredients of his daily life. He may not worry too much about lack of schools for his children and may never have seen the inside of a modern hospital. His apparatus for living may be of the simplest. And yet, in planning for his repatriation or resettlement the difference between his material requirements and those of the European refugee must not be exaggerated.

Knowing only of the extremely low remuneration of oriental labor, the hard work and primitive living conditions of the great peasant majority, the Occidental may easily imagine that in his needs and feelings and desires the Oriental is a being very different from himself. Yet, the humble Chinese, Korean, Malay, or Filipino is no less attached to his home than the European; having so little else of comfort and enjoyment, he loves even more his thatched hut and his little plot of land. And although it may be true that those reared in a warm climate can sustain life on "a handful of rice," with but few other ingredients, it by no means follows that they care to see their children lose flesh and die from lack of a more health-giving diet. They may be patient—incredibly patient from the Occidental's standpoint; but those who habitually dwell close to the zero line of subsistence sometimes rise with surprising courage and vigor when life itself is at stake. They will not meekly submit to fate if inefficiency

182

or corruption should, after the enemy's defeat, delay that return to normal home life to which they consider themselves entitled.

It is important to anticipate such reactions as these, because they bear on international policy. It is sometimes said that repatriation of the homeless is not as great a task in eastern Asia as it is in Europe because the people are accustomed to walk long distances, their few possessions slung from a carrying pole, accustomed to put up with every conceivable hardship on the way. It would be dangerous, I think, to plan and act upon that view. In global planning beware of the rationalization of racial prejudice. Heir of a thousand skills which the world can ill spare, heir, too, of many of those inventions which, further developed with modern techniques, now implement our lives, the Asiatic has no less a claim on our common resources than has the European.

The emergency task will be greatest in China which will have been at war for at least eight years. No one, apparently, can foretell with any assurance what the return flow of population from Free China to what is now Occupied China will be in the period immediately following the re-occupation of the Yangtze Valley and of the southern provinces. There has already been a sizable drift back. Whether this drift will swell to the dimensions of a flood depends to some extent on the power of the national government to control it. And this, again, involves its financial ability to implement the plans which it has made for the development of new industrial centers and new means of transportation. When the war ends, the equipment of the western provinces for industrial production still will be no match to that in Kiangsu, Chekiang, or Kwangtung. Nearness to foreign markets and supply of skilled labor, plant and machinery ready for use, still are economic assets which no government policy can disregard.

We must reckon, then, with a sizable return movement of people to the coastal provinces. And this movement is likely to involve millions. But its volume and speed will largely depend on the circumstances under which the war ends—for example, whether the enemy will have a chance to commit wholesale destruction before he is forced to leave, whether perhaps the military operations of the United Nations themselves necessitate a strategy of "scorched earth."

There certainly will be a serious relief problem in the port cities. The arrival of food ships, following upon re-occupation, cannot be kept secret and must be expected to stimulate the coastward migration. Lack of transportation facilities in China makes it difficult to regulate the flow of migrants, though it sets a limit to the speed of any migratory movement. Half-hearted attempts at regulation might produce eddies and added confusion, while a well conceived working plan, administered by officers of experience and equipped with adequate legal power, would help to relieve the pressure on the eastern cities.

There are always possibilities also of the recurrence, before order has been restored, of floods and droughts, hence famines like that in 1942 which drove millions of peasants from their homes in Honan across the Yellow River and the inhospitable Sin Ling Mountains (see above, p. 39). Resentment of conscription of man power and military exactions, too, may continue to produce migrations of some magnitude and difficult to bring under control.

In other countries of eastern Asia, likewise, events yet to come and now hard to foresee, may produce migratory movements other than those of a straight repatriation. Mention has been made above (p. 96) of the unknown tendencies of Korean expatriates. Will many of them wish to return to their homeland as soon as it has been freed of Japanese rule? Will they be permitted to do so until opportunities for their livelihood and orderly settlement have been created? In the now occupied countries of Southeast Asia, unemployment in the cities will be the chief emergency problem at the time of recovery. Extreme poverty must be expected to prevail among the alien Asiatics who live in cities and whose normal functions as makers and distributors of consumer goods to the native people will have been interrupted for a long time.

Taking the region as a whole, the displacement of population is only one element in a disturbance of normal life which varies in intensity with local conditions and the impact of the war. Relief and rehabilitation call for an economical use of all available resources, human energy no less than supplies from outside and the gifts of nature. But the uprooting of so many people from their homes or from their accustomed occupations affords opportunities of social readjustment as well as problems. Millions of people who have known only tradition with all its limitations on material progress can, under appropriate policies, be set free to build for their children a happier future. But this requires a co-ordination of the immediate relief plans with the larger plans for redressing the historic lack of balance between population and resources.

The Need for Concerted Planning

THERE IS NEED, then, for planning, and this primarily in relation to possibilities of strengthening the economic position of peoples and population groups where they are at home. Larger production—and a larger share of the masses in the product, larger and more remunerative opportunities of trade, more economic uses of local resources, more equitable taxation, efforts to stabilize price levels and currencies, and many other factors can be utilized to reduce the need for recourse to emigration, whether in search of a new domicile or in search of temporary employment. For this reason if for no other, many concerns heretofore generally regarded as domestic now have their larger recognized international implications. One cannot fruitfully discuss policies of migration and resettlement in a void, as though they had no connection with other problems of statecraft, national and international.

However, in addition to these larger vistas of involvement there are also, as we have seen, many specific and even technical tasks for concerted planning. To those already mentioned two more might be added here. Both have to do with increased mobility. The first suggestion is that the difficult working and living conditions which exist in the most densely populated parts of eastern Asia can, in some instances, best be improved by providing transportation facilities which will enable some of the people, those whose labor is required during a few months of the year only—as, for example, in rice planting and harvesting—to live somewhere, not too far away, on higher ground and there, on land of admittedly lesser fertility, to engage in mixed farming and seasonal industries, dovetailing with their occupation in the wet lowlands. Another suggestion, already intimated (p. 150), is

185

that larger numbers of native residents in tropical lands might be given the opportunity of renewing their health and physical vigor by spending a time in the Temperate Zone. This is not as utopian as it may sound. Thousands of young Malays, for example, might be drawn into the international armed forces which henceforth will police the world. They might be drawn from the most densely populated districts in Java and the Philippines, many of them to settle, upon their return, on the more sparsely populated islands. Some of the labor recruiting for great international work projects in the Temperate Zone may deliberately be done, too, in tropical countries, so as to give yet more young people the chance of spending a few years of their life in a more invigorating climate. Connected with such matters as these and vital to population policy, although rarely discussed in this connection, is the whole question of public health. We have counted noses and we have counted mouths to feed when we inquired into the relation of population density to the supporting capacity of a given area. We should ask ourselves also how the people themselves might be made more productive by better protection against devitalizing parasites and fevers. In the more northern lands of eastern Asia a comparable demand on public policy in connection with agrarian reforms is that of applying those remedies to malnutrition which spring from social and economic incongruities rather than from a basic disproportion between population and arable acreage.

These are some of the tasks for concerted international action. Only through forming the habit of working together on specific problems of population pressure, of migration, and of resettlement, will the nations learn eventually to deal in common also with the greatest of all international social problems, the differential growth of populations. Below the thin veneer of civilization the old struggle for survival continues. It will no doubt continue for many generations; but in the light of new knowledge and inspired by new social purpose it need not remain a blind struggle. The head-hunting tribesman only knows that it is customary, natural, and divinely sanctioned to regard the people in the next valley as aliens and rivals. The Burmese nationalist thinks of the need for survival primarily as it affects his own language group. Racial and religious minorities cling—

186

often fanatically—to concepts of group identity which, objectively considered, have little reality in the every-day life of the individuals who compose them. For, although the cultural divisions still play a genuine role in the pattern of oriental society, they have been overlaid by a network of new relationships more closely associated with livelihood and security. We must not underestimate the desire of all men to continue the accustomed mode of life, to be guided by the established moral and aesthetic sanctions; and from this desire spring conflicts that may lead to war. But such conflicts are more certain to become virulent if the concern for the preservation of the inherited culture is tinged with fear by the excessive growth in number or economic power of the contending groups. Lasting peace will not be attained until that fear is laid by a democratic international concern with the distribution of population.

As yet, few peoples or self-conscious population groups would be willing to share with others any determination of the extent to which, or the means by which, they will attain the certainty of their own survival. Progress toward such collaboration can come only from work on specific common problems such as those mentioned above. And even that progress, in the present temper of the world, is likely to be slow. There is one field of action, however, that cannot wait. Distinct from the larger questions of policy is the question of aid and refuge for the war-dislocated people of the world. In the present study we have touched only on some aspects of that question: all of them lead back to more fundamental problems which sooner or later must be faced by a permanent international body established for that purpose.

The case for an international agency specifically to deal with the more immediate problems of migration has been amply made by Paul van Zeeland, the former Prime Minister of Belgium, and others.[2] This agency requires a regional set-up if the particular tasks created in different parts of the world by the composition of their populations and the nature of their needs are to be sufficiently recognized. And it seems inevitable that it

[2] *Post-war Migrations; Proposals for an International Agency*, American Jewish Committee, New York, 1943, 54 pp. See also *Annals of the Academy of Political and Social Science*, Vol. 235 (July, 1944).

concern itself not only with the distribution of refugees but also with their care and supervision in transit and the mutual responsibilities between sending and receiving countries. Moreover, it would seem imperative that some international standards be set, and perhaps enforced by international regional agreements, for the subsequent protection of resettled groups and individuals, and for the protection of foreign capital invested in resettlement projects.

The respective roles to be played and the instrumentalities to be provided by international agencies now existing or yet to be created will require considerations outside the frame of the present study. The Inter-Governmental Committee on Refugees, the United Nations Relief and Rehabilitation Administration, and the International Labor Organization are involved; each of them already has made contributions toward the advance of the common aim.[3] The International Red Cross and many private institutions will continue to implement discussion and policy with the findings of first-hand studies, such as some of those referred to on previous pages. As postwar planning under public and private auspices gains in sureness and precision, it will be found that it is possible and necessary to separate somewhat the immediate tasks from the larger task of exerting a democratic world control over the hitherto chaotic migration movements that have their source in the unequal distribution of the world's material resources.

War, we have seen, is only a link in a chain of events which goes back to ancient conquests and to accidental historic changes in the respective power position of peoples. Such a chain can be broken by constructive statesmanship. Migration, whether internal or international, is an instrument of equalization. As such it acts almost automatically when it is not artificially impeded. But it can became the instrument of something even better than equalization, an instrument for raising the productive ability of men. The profit motive in pre-war days has shipped men like cattle to use their muscle only and to degrade their intelligence. Little attention has been paid to the effect of unplanned human

[3] See *The Relocation of Uprooted Peoples*, National Planning Association, Washington, D. C., pamphlet, 1944.

reproduction on the success of planned changes in their distribu
tion. The motive of public service so strongly emphasized in the
declared war aims of the United Nations will help to adjust
population and resources so that all men will gain a decent
living and be relatively secure.

APPENDIX

INDIAN EMIGRATION BEYOND ASIA

ALTHOUGH IT FALLS outside the scope of the present study, the author has been asked to add a statement about the outlook for Indian labor emigration to countries outside of Asia, because Indians may be thought of as in competition, in many parts of the world, with workers coming from eastern Asiatic countries. In the South Pacific, Fiji is the only dependency where Indians are a substantial labor force. Ninety-two thousand strong, they made up 43.8 per cent of the total population in 1938, but there had been no active immigration movement for some years. They were employed mainly in the sugar industry as cane cutters and mill laborers, both of them seasonal occupations, representing the remnant of large labor forces formerly recruited for the West Indies and from 1879 on, after the British annexation of Fiji, diverted to that archipelago. With the ending of the indentured labor system, about 1920, some thousands of Indian workers stayed on and set up families, so that a stable Indian labor reserve seems assured for the future—especially since employment conditions have greatly improved in recent years.[1]

In the countries of the Occident, Indian labor immigration is, of course, excluded, as is that of other Asiatics. Nevertheless, a recent enumeration of Indians in foreign lands comes to the total of 3,768,000. Included are 1,018,000 in Burma, 745,000 in Malaya, and 800,000 in Ceylon. Away from the Asiatic mainland, the largest Indian populations are those of Mauritius (270,000), Natal (184,000), Trinidad (161,100), British Guiana (143,000).

[1] *Annual Reports on the Social and Economic Progress of the People of Fiji*, 1935-38, H. M. Stationery Office, London; Felix M. Keesing, *The South Seas in the Modern World*, New York, 1941, pp. 277-82.

Fiji comes next (95,000), then Kenya (45,000), Dutch Guiana (41,000), the Transvaal (26,000), Tanganyika (23,000), Jamaica (19,000).[2] The total number of Indians in the United States, in 1940, was only 2,405 (as against 5,350 in 1930). In the Philippines there are only about a thousand, in Canada 1,500.

Originally, the mass emigration of Indians to other parts of the Pacific and across the Indian Ocean was, like that of Chinese, mainly for purposes of contract labor in large European-owned enterprises; and the conditions of indentured Indian labor were no whit better. The present distribution of the Indian emigrant population, while it somewhat reflects that original purpose, also indicates, however, the extent to which it has been able to assume other economic functions. More especially, Indian immi‹ grants in different parts of Africa have been able to insinuate themselves between the native peasantry and the European merchants as a middle class with a recognized place in society. A further rise in social status, and the development of important industries in India, however, has led to a growing sense of competition between European and Indian importers and retail merchants, and a corresponding growth of restrictions upon the freedom of Indians, including those of the second and third generations.

In South Africa the rising antagonisms toward the residents of Indian descent has led to a ghetto-like system of segregation which, like that enforced upon Jews in Czarist Russia, has produced a number of undesirable traits which again have become the ostensible reasons for further discriminations. Moreover, in neither case has it ever been possible fully to enforce all the prohibitions; and the minority, restricted in its freedom in some particulars, has been able to develop its economic life along lines even more disturbing to the country's welfare than would have been its free exercise of choice in vocation and residence.

[2] *The Indian Year Book, 1942-1943,* Bombay, 1943, pp. 879-80. There is no recent estimate for the number of Indians in Thailand; in 1931 it was about 55,000 and it has since decreased. For a descriptive "survey of the problems of Indians in foreign lands" see Dharam Yash Dev, *Our Countrymen Abroad,* with a foreword by Jawaharlal Nehru, All India Congress Committee, Allahabad, 1940; and C. F. Andrews, *India and the Pacific,* London, 1937.

For nearly a hundred years the Indian problem has been the occasion for violent displays of racial emotion. It has been the reason for more commissions and select committees than any other topic, and mass legislation affecting it includes more than 60 Acts of Parliament and provincial ordinances. Broadly the problem has its origin in the demand of the Natal sugar planters in the middle of the last century for that cheap labor which the warrior Zulu was not prepared to give. Then began the system of indentured labour which lasted from 1860 to 1911 and has left this country with more than 250,000 Indians, over 80 per cent of them born in South Africa.[3]

Incidentally, the reported inability of the South African government fully to enforce the residential segregation against Indians makes it unlikely that the Burmese and the Thai governments will fare much better if after the war they should continue to seek to protect themselves against the competition of Indian and Chinese residents of long standing through restrictive legislation rather than through friendly agreement with the Indian and Chinese governments.

In Australia, even though the "White Australia" policy has almost become a religious dogma, race prejudice in every-day relations is much less pronounced than in Africa. But this is a result of the early date at which restrictive legislation was adopted, so that a large immigration of Asiatics could not take place. The 2,400 Indians counted in the Australian census of 1933 were for the most part engaged in business.

An Indian community consisting mostly of manual workers engenders hostility only when its energies are concentrated on occupations in which they compete with natives. Thus J. D. Tyson, a representative of the Indian government, sent to the West Indies for preparatory studies to implement a Royal Commission of Enquiry, reported in 1939:

Compared with the East Indian communities in British Guiana and Trinidad, I found the East Indians of Jamaica backward as a community and very helpless, numbering among them barely a dozen professional men and merchants, practically no civil servants or even teachers, and having outside Kingston no organisation and no acknowledged leaders.[4]

[3] "South Africa, I. The Indian Problem," *The Round Table*, 131 (June, 1943), 288.

[4] Dharam Yash Dev, *op. cit.*, p. 38.

The Indians of Canada are a small remnant of much larger
numbers attracted from the Punjab in the first decade of this
century—twelve to fifteen thousand—by the development of the
lumber industry in British Columbia. Their competition was
resented by European lumbermen, and a more general opposition to them flared up during the First World War when some
Indian leaders took an independent stand on international affairs
and suspicion of the loyalty of Indian immigrants became widespread. Most of these were driven out by a series of bloody
encounters and through legalistic and unfair court decisions.
Since they were British subjects, indirect legislation was resorted to in order to prevent further immigration of Indians,
even at their own initiative and expense. Today the small Indian
population of Canada, practically all Sikhs from the Punjab, are
farmers in the Okanagan and Fraser Valleys of British Columbia.
Some who have prospered in the lumber business now run their
own mills, but many more are wage-earners in the lumber and
fuel industries. Although British subjects and, many of them,
army veterans, they are refused naturalization.[5]

No demographic or social study of the equally small Indian
population in the United States seems ever to have been made.
They are in origin identical with the Canadian Indians, and
indeed many of them entered the continent by a British Colum-
bian port. They were by experience and previous way of life
more suited for work in the growing fruit and vegetable industry
of California than for the cold Canadian forests. Many of them
at first secured employment in railroad construction when they
drifted over the Canadian border. Although their number never
exceeded a few thousand, war-time emotions exaggerated the
danger of an Indian mass infiltration, and the Immigration Act
of 1917 with its complete prohibition of immigration from an
arbitrarily fixed "barred zone" in southern Asia was directed in
the main against Indians. Like other Asiatics, Indians continued
to be entirely excluded from the right to enter the United States

[5] Sadhu Singh Dhami, *The Sikhs and Their Religion*, Khalsa Divan
Society, Vancouver and Victoria, 1943, p. 24; Sripati Chandrasekhar, *The
Population Problem in India*, New York, in the press, Chapter VI.

when that Act was amended by the quota provisions of the Immigration Act of 1924.[6]

Today, the largest Indian community in the United States is that of agricultural workers in the vicinity of Stockton, California, where their sturdy qualities have long been recognized more especially in the growing of asparagus and in the maintenance of irrigation systems; but most of them are now dispersed over that state. Largely because of the presence in the United States of Indian university students and business men, the influence of this national minority on public opinion is much larger than its numbers might suggest.

There is no likelihood that any of the countries that have received Indian immigrants in the past will open their doors widely to them after the war. Some concessions may be made, like those already made in Burma, to improve the status of Indians long resident and identified with the interests of the country in which they live. But in every case where they have come in substantial numbers, there has been a particular occasion and cause for their admission; and in the meantime conditions have changed. There no longer is an active demand for Indian labor except in countries close to India.

Whether India is "overpopulated" is a moot question over which much ink has been spilled.[7] What is certain is that the growth of India's population at the present rate constitutes a danger to future peace unless relief is afforded either by emigration or by an unprecedented development of the country's internal resources and the birth-rate is reduced by every known device.

Every day India adds to her population the equivalent of at least a town of twenty-four thousand inhabitants. This means that India's population increases every year by at least five millions. According to the census taken on March 1, 1941, India's population was 388,800,000. Today it must have reached the mark of four hundred millions.[8]

[6] For a history of Indian immigration to the United States and the effects of the legislation mentioned in the text, see S. Chandrasekhar, *op. cit.*, Chapter VI.

[7] See for example S. Chandrasekhar, "Population Pressure in India," *Pacific Affairs*, XVI, 2 (June, 1943), 166-84.

[8] S. Chandrasekhar, "Growth and Characteristics of India's Population," *Scientific Monthly*, July, 1943. See also Warren S. Thompson, *op. cit.*, p. 95.

India's population shows a trend toward a reduced rate of increase, but this may not be large enough tc offset the influences that continue to pull in the opposite direction: extreme poverty, ignorance, and the tradition-bound social attitudes of the great majority. The present occasion does not permit of an extended discussion either of the factors that make India a danger spot in world population or of the incipient forces, similar to those in other oriental countries, that make for an adjustment of population growth to actual resources. For the immediate future the economic and demographic reality of India affords no cheerful prospect.

Indian emigration to all parts of eastern Asia has, of course, ceased for the time being. Its future will depend on the state of political international relations after the war, which is not now predictable. However, one or two tendencies may be indicated. There is likely to be continued antagonism toward the Indian immigrant on two counts: competition for employment and the sharp practices of Indian middlemen. Indian emigration to Burma and Thailand, more especially, may be expected to be further reduced, rather than expanded, by means of agreements and unilateral regulations. British Malaya, on the other hand, would be dependent on Indian labor if rubber estates were to resume production in full strength at the end of the war. Only if a much stronger conflict should develop between the Indian and British governments than that of the past would the Malayan employers be forced to abandon their Indian labor supply and replace it, probably, with Javanese labor. They consider the latter less reliable and more expensive. To be entirely cut off from employment opportunities in British Malaya would be a serious loss for Madras; and this would be especially so if, under the impetus of the new social policies implied in the declared war aims of the United Nations and implemented by the International Labor Conference at its twenty-sixth session, in 1944, there were going to be a considerable further improvement in the working and living conditions of plantation laborers. Even at best, the outlook for southern India is dismal. Increased opportunities for temporary labor migration cannot bring genuine relief of population pressure unless they are accompanied by far-reaching long-term programs of economic reconstruction.

INDEX

aborigines, protection of, 159-60, 165

absentee landlordism, 9-10, 19, 20, 37, 81, 180

Africa, Chinese in, 168; Indians in, 167, 191, 192, 193; oriental exclusion, 167

air travel, 112, 171

Alunan, Rafael, 149

America, migration to, 3-4; *see also* Brazil, Canada, Latin America, Peru, United States

Amoy, 42, 57, 74, 130

Andrews, C. F., 192

Andrus, J. Russell, 14, 29

Angelo, A. C., 165

Anhwei, 8, 13, 38

Annamite emigration, 17, 28, 58, 67-8

Arabs in southeast Asia, 63-4

Australia, Chinese in, 72, 73, 75, 83; Indians in, 193; Jewish colonization, 164-5; land uses, 162; oriental exclusion, 161 ff., 174; population capacity, 162, 163, 166

banditry, effect of, 9, 10, 18, 37, 87, 89, 90

Barnett, Patricia C., 130

Barnett, Robert W., 11, 106

Beard, Miriam, 139

Bell, Minnie, 164

Belshaw, Horace, 166

Birobidzhan, 48

birth rates, 11-12 (*see also* population growth, *also* subhead under various countries)

Boeke, J. H., 81, 146

Borneo, 16, 17, 18, 27, 58, 73, 81, 112, 113, 145, 178

Borsodi, Ralph, 119

Bouthoul, Gaston, 165

Bowman, Isaiah, 114

Brazil, Chinese in, 73; Japanese in, 108

Broek, Jan O. M., 66, 114, 146

Buck, John Lossing, 116, 131

Burma, Chinese in, 42, 73, 79-81, 149; crafts, 34, 148; effect of war and occupation on, 29-30, 33, 34, 62, 148; imports, 137; independence movement 30, 148; Indians in, 29, 34, 58, 60-3, 148, 149, 191, 195, 196; industrialization, 147-8; international labor resources, 148; land utilization, 148; migration, 33; natural resources, 6, 148; population density, 14; population growth, 14; rice exports, 29, 38, 148; taxation, 29; vital statistics, 14

Burma Road, 80

Burma-Yunnan Railroad, 80

Butler, Harold, 60

Canada, Chinese in, 72, 73, 174; Indians in, 192, 194

197